I DIDN'T WANT TO DIE,

I JUST WANTED THE PAIN TO END

Praise for *I Didn't Want to Die, I Just Wanted the Pain to End.*

"Incredibly vulnerable, epically raw and unbelievably inspiring. Shane connects honestly within to the little boy terrified of himself and the man struggling to find peace of mind. I've never wanted to run and sit in the darkness, under the bed and, in the cupboard, with someone so badly. It was absolutely heartbreaking to feel the utter loneliness of suicidal ideation. This is the book that will let the little kid in all of us know, eventually, and with enough work, it will all be okay, even when it's not."

— Tenille, psychologist, Victoria, Australia

"Shane's book is an amazing representation of hard work, self-reflection, dedication and compassion.

As I read the book, no matter what I was going through during the time, each time I picked the book up, it seemed to always have the perfect advice or encapsulate exactly how I was feeling when I needed it. 'I want every single human to feel like they are somebody, because every human deserves that', was a favourite quote within the book. I wholeheartedly believe each person who reads Shane's story will feel less alone and more connected, allowing each reader to feel they are somebody. This is a credit to Shane's down-to-earth and real perspective towards mental health and how to best cope both as an individual struggling and as a support of someone else.

By sharing his story with such truth and passion, Shane undoubtedly has created something special that will provide hope to others and break down the stigma of mental health issues."

— Georgina, Victoria, Australia

I DIDN'T WANT TO DIE, I JUST WANTED THE PAIN TO END

FINDING A BETTER WAY

SHANE KELTON

First published in 2023 by Dean Publishing
PO Box 119
Mt. Macedon, Victoria, 3441
Australia
deanpublishing.com

Copyright © Shane Kelton

All rights reserved. No part of this publication may be reproduced, stored in a retrieval system or transmitted in any way or by any means, electronic, mechanical, photocopying, recording or otherwise, without the prior written permission of the publisher.

Cataloguing-in-Publication Data
National Library of Australia
Title: I Didn't Want To Die, I Just Wanted The Pain To End
Edition: 1st edn
ISBN: 978-1-925452-70-9
Category: NONFICTION/Self-help/memoir

The stories in this book reflect the author's recollection of events. Some names, locations, and identifying characteristics have been changed to protect the privacy of those depicted.

Dialogue and some encounters or experiences have been recreated from the author's memory. This book deals with mental health, mental illness and suicidal thoughts. Some themes may be confronting and troubling for some readers so discretion is advised.

This book is part memoir and is not meant to be used, nor should it be used, to diagnose or treat any physical, emotional, or psychological medical condition. For diagnosis or treatment of any medical problem, consult your own physician. The publisher and author are not responsible for any specific health or psychological needs that may require medical supervision and are not liable for any damages or negative consequences from any treatment, action, application, or preparation to any person reading or following the information in this book. References are provided for informational purposes only and do not constitute endorsement of any websites or other sources. Neither the publisher nor the individual author(s) shall be liable for any physical, psychological, emotional, financial, or commercial damages, including, but not limited to, special, incidental, consequential, or other damages. Our views and rights are the same: You are responsible for your own choices, actions, and results. The author encourages anyone who needs help, to seek professional help immediately and advocate for their mental, physical and emotional help.

This book details the author's opinion and personal experiences only and does not represent professionals health advice.

Dedication

Writing my story and sharing my journey to help others was something I always wanted to do, but something held me back. That was until October of 2022, when I got a call at 9:30 on a Saturday morning to say that an amazing young man was found dead. Another young man struggling with an internal battle I was so lucky to survive had passed. It was enough for me to say, "I have to do this now." Because I don't want that feeling again, and I don't want to see so many of the people I love hurting.

This book is dedicated to Bryn, Emma, Kynan, Camdyn, and Shayla Jones. Kynan will never be forgotten and while he doesn't get to share his story, I will continue to share mine in his honour and for all the people we have lost to the tragedy that is suicide.

Kynan – you are someone I and many others will miss. The cheeky smile, the cheeky attitude, with such an amazing, caring heart.

This book is dedicated to all the individuals and families who have been involved in mental illness battles. It has a ripple effect across communities. To those who we don't get to see smile anymore, we miss you.

This book is dedicated to everyone who has felt or is feeling lost, scared, and alone, battling in the depths of mental health struggles. I want you and those around you to have hope that happiness and health in your life is possible. YOU ARE WORTH IT!

I also want to dedicate this book to all those who have lost loved ones to mental health struggles. Those we have lost are the driving force for change within me. Where possible, I want to prevent the pain that the individuals, the friends, and the families go through.

CONTENTS

INTRODUCTION: I'M AN OPEN BOOK xi

CHAPTER 1: WHEN I KNEW I COULD HELP 1

CHAPTER 2: A PRETTY NORMAL CHILDHOOD 9

CHAPTER 3: EARLY TEENAGE YEARS
AND WANTING TO DIE 15

CHAPTER 4: LATE TEENAGE YEARS
- THE STRUGGLE INTENSIFIES 25

CHAPTER 5: MY SUICIDE ATTEMPT 49

CHAPTER 6: THE JOURNEY TO BEING OKAY 63

CHAPTER 7: WHAT I HAVE LEARNT 93

CHAPTER 8: HOW TO HELP YOURSELF 121

CHAPTER 9: FOR THE CAREGIVERS 173

CHAPTER 10: WHERE TO GO FROM HERE
- MY GOALS FOR MENTAL HEALTH 211

CONCLUSION: WHAT MORE CAN I SAY? 233

ACKNOWLEDGEMENTS 238

IMPORTANT RESOURCES 240

ABOUT THE AUTHOR 241

INTRODUCTION

I'M AN OPEN BOOK

"Are you okay?" The voice came through my open car door.

As I came to, I responded, "If this is real life, then no, I'm not."

I'd survived my first suicide attempt at the age of 21. But how did I get to this point?

Your dream might be different to mine. We all have these dreams, but they are either achieved or not achieved so often due to our own health, our own choices, and the environments we can control. This book will take you through the journey of how my mental health issues, from anxiety to depression and suicide attempts, held me back from achieving what I wanted in life. The rollercoaster that life is took me to the depths of extreme suffering on many occasions, and I hope this book can give you the skills to change your life, help someone else change theirs, or just give that little bit of hope that things will turn around.

I really want people who might be struggling to walk into a bookstore, see this book, and use it to help themselves. You might be waiting to get into a psychologist, or you might just be having a hard day, and knowledge is a lifeline. I know so many people who have had books help them. The knowledge they got went straight into their minds and hearts, and it became really important to them.

I want to be someone anyone can come to and talk to because they feel comfortable and know I'm there to listen and help. I want my book to be an extension of that – I can be with people in a different way, and I can help them feel like they're not alone and that they belong. I know you and understand you because I've been there and felt the same way. I want to nurture you and be honest and up front. Personally, I'm still learning how to manage my emotions and be emotional when this stuff comes up – it's a constant process.

I hope this book opens up people's abilities to have these conversations about mental health. That's my dream. I was so tentative about being open about that dream because I feared that people might think it came from a place of ego, but I know, truthfully, this isn't about me. This is about you, our community, and society. I just want to help people feel better.

CHAPTER 1

WHEN I KNEW I COULD HELP

A GUT FEELING I COULDN'T IGNORE

The first time I supported someone who was suicidal, I was 18 years old. It was late at night on New Year's Eve of 2006, around 8 or 9 pm, and my mate, Troy, and I were running along the beach at Mornington Peninsula to meet some girls. I was intoxicated, and not just on alcohol but also on the energy of the night. I had spent the day with good friends; I was going to meet a girl who I really liked, and soon we would all be sitting on the beach, watching as fireworks signalled the start of a new year, a new beginning.

New Year's was always my favourite time of year, but not for the reasons you might think. Whenever the new year arrived, I breathed a sigh of relief and felt grateful that I was still here. I had survived another year. Would I make it through another 12 months? Considering my daily suicidal thoughts, I couldn't say for sure, but it didn't matter. What mattered on New Year's Eve, as I drank and laughed with my mates, was that I was here now. I had lived to see another year. Looking back, being happy to make it through another year without killing myself wasn't the positive attitude I thought it was at the time.

As I ran along the beach, supercharged with excitement, no one could have guessed that I frequently battled suicidal thoughts. No one could have guessed that earlier that night, I'd had a massive meltdown in front of my mates. No one could have guessed the truth. Let's go back to earlier in the night…

Being 18, New Year's Eve was about drinking as much as possible. Your ability to drink defined your strength. Were you hard enough to keep up with your mates? Or were you too soft to drink to excess, a lightweight? Well, I certainly didn't want people to think I was soft, so, let's say, I knocked back more than a few alcoholic beverages that night.

Eventually, things turned sour, as they quite often did when I drank. At that time, I wasn't equipped to deal with my emotions, and I often acted on impulse. As you'll soon understand, the positions I put myself in weren't beneficial for me or the people around me. When that switch flipped, I could bring down the mood and ruin everyone's day in an instant.

During the day, we were drinking on a vacant block of land adjacent to where a friend's family had hired a holiday house, and, in my intoxicated state, I dropped my phone and smashed the screen. It was completely unusable. For me, it was the end of the world. I had been messaging the girl I was interested in, but, without a phone, I now had no way to contact her. What would she think? Would she think I wasn't interested anymore? Would she find someone else? *Shit*, I had to do something.

As the negative thoughts spiralled around inside my head, I felt like I was losing control. In truth, I *was* losing control, of my thoughts *and* my actions. My mum was staying somewhere close by, so I made the quick and pretty stupid decision to sneak off, grab my car keys from my bag, and walk to my car. The plan was to take the SIM card out of my phone and put it in Mum's. The thing is, plenty of my mates had phones, so I don't know why I felt like I had to drink drive my way to a solution. Whatever my reasoning at the time, I had a plan, and I was determined to see it through. There was no way I was letting a broken phone ruin my chances with the girl I liked. Was I thinking logically? Not by a long shot. But in my head, everything I was doing made sense. I said earlier that I felt like I was losing control, but, really, I was losing the ability to think clearly and see reason, which is practically the same thing.

Thankfully, before I managed to get in my car, my mates realised what I was doing and stepped in to stop me. Although I'm thankful now, at the time, I was far from pleased. In fact, I was furious. *How dare they try to stop me? Don't they know what's at stake?* I yelled and swore and, quite frankly, made a bit of a scene. Some of a friend's family members also got involved, trying to reason with me – but I wasn't having it. I just couldn't stand the thought of being without a phone for an entire night. *Anything could happen in that time. She'll meet another guy, for sure. Fuck!* No one in their right mind was going to let me drive in the state I was in, and the frustration boiled over. I was so pissed off at my mates but instead of taking it out on them physically, I made the somewhat better but still stupid decision to punch my own windscreen. I didn't break the glass, but my hand wasn't in great shape afterwards. Not that I could feel much at the time, but the pain and stiff knuckles served as a constant reminder of my behaviour for weeks to come.

Unfortunately, this wasn't the first time I had acted like this. My mates had seen me in similar states many times before. One minute, I would be fine. The next minute, I would be having a total meltdown and taking out my frustrations on everyone and everything around me. Looking back, I was filled with fear and negative beliefs about myself. Mainly, I thought I wasn't good enough, and I had no idea how to deal with these self-sabotaging thoughts and feelings. So, when I felt like I had no control over a situation, I lost control, which is a bit ironic, yeah?

Ultimately, after punching my windscreen and abandoning my plan to drink drive, which, looking back, had no chance of ending well, my friend's parents were able to calm me down. Considering my state of mind, they took the perfect approach. The entire time, they observed the situation without judgement and came up with a solution. They would drive me to get a phone the next day, and, in the meantime, I could use a friend's phone to text the girl. Simple. Sensible. Smart. Why didn't I think of that?

What no one saw were my well-hidden suicidal thoughts, self-esteem issues, internal hatred of who I was, and the fact that I had been living with those thoughts for five years. That year, as I worked my way through year 12, I had battled more suicidal thoughts than ever before. To me, the year was a success because I had survived countless nights of wanting to end my life. On nights where I planned to end it, I reached out to friends, and, every time, I survived to see the morning. If those friends had not been there for me when I needed them, well, it scares me to imagine what might have happened. Of course, I rarely told anyone exactly what I was going through. Few people knew the extent of my suicidal thoughts.

After the situation simmered down, my mood improved, and we all walked down to the beach, which was where Troy told me the girl I liked was coming to meet us. Suddenly, the fears, the insecurities, the throbbing in my hand didn't matter. My luck had finally changed!

As I rushed along the beach, trailing behind Troy, to meet the girls, something caught my eye. A girl was sitting on the sand, crying loudly and uncontrollably. Her friend was sitting beside her, trying to calm her down, but the girl was inconsolable. Something inside me compelled me to stop – so I did. Troy told me to leave it and keep going. Why would I stop for a random girl? The girl I liked was waiting for me down the beach. I couldn't stand her up… But an instinct, a gut feeling, told me I had to stop and help this girl, who was clearly in distress.

"What's wrong?" I asked.

The girl continued to cry.

"I'll meet you at the spot," Troy said, reassessing the situation and giving me his support to help the person in need. He continued along the beach, while I stayed.

The girl's friend looked to me. "She said she wants to kill herself. I can't… I don't know what to do."

Without thinking, I clicked into gear, sitting beside the distressed girl, who wanted to end her life. Until that moment, I had mostly kept my suicidal thoughts to myself, but I didn't think twice about opening up to this random girl, who was feeling the same pain I had felt for the last five years.

I shared my own struggles and explained that, only hours ago, I was in a rage and wanted to end my life too. I told her she wasn't alone and the thoughts she was having didn't control her. After about ten minutes, her shoulders relaxed, and the tears began to clear from her eyes. Eventually, the girl started to share small parts of her story, and we bounced some ideas off each other. Sharing my own struggles felt natural, not selfish as I had thought it would. It felt like there was a purpose to what I was saying, what I was doing, and, honestly, it felt good. It felt good to let it all out, but it felt even better to see the relief in the girl and her friend. By stopping and giving this girl my time and attention, I made a difference, a *real* difference.

We all stood, and her friend thanked me.

I met the girl's sad but hopeful eyes. "Are you okay now?"

"Yes… yes, I'm okay now."

I trusted her words, so I said my goodbyes and continued along the beach. Before I knew it, I was running again, exhilarated by the moment of vulnerability I had shared with that random girl and the good that had come from it. It was such a key moment in my life because I realised then that sharing my story wasn't selfish. It was selfless and powerful. It was strong and valuable. It allowed me to relate to that girl and help her in her moment of need.

I don't know if she is alive today, but I hope our conversation motivated her to reach out for further help. I hope, as she said, she's okay now.

You see, I didn't save her. You can't save anyone. While you may be able to hold people back, it's only a temporary solution. To identify and address the root cause of their issues, they need to do the work themselves. We can guide them, absolutely, but we can't save them. They can only save themselves.

After that experience on the beach, I understood the power of authenticity, and I got my first inkling that maybe I had a purpose in this life. Ultimately, a horror day turned into one of the most significant nights of my life.

CHAPTER 2

A PRETTY NORMAL CHILDHOOD

A LIFE FULL OF LOVE

I'd say my childhood was pretty normal. As far as I remember, Mum and Dad were amazing parents, who set boundaries, worked hard, and did everything they could to help us grow, develop, and learn.

I was born in Melbourne in 1988, and my brother, Steven, came along in 1990. We grew up in a typical family home, and home life was fun. I remember, from a very young age, playing board games with fish 'n' chips or lawn bowls or footy in the hallway, and there was plenty of backyard sport with my brother in the suburbs.

For as long as I can remember, Mum and Dad both worked full-time. We weren't well-off, but we weren't struggling either.

From what I recall, the first few years of my childhood were filled with love.

While my brother and I got along well for the most part, we fought quite often too. I would fill with jealousy when my friends hung out with him, and we would argue when I refused to be out in backyard cricket. Regardless, I had so much love for him, and, as my journey unfolded, it was hard seeing him upset and angry with who I sometimes became.

UNEARTHING MY TRAUMA

Recently, during a trauma session with my therapist, I discovered a memory of what I thought was sexual abuse from a family member. However, the reality of the situation was that when I was three, that family member was tickling me. I was trying to get them off me, and I wet myself.

Because I wet myself when I felt stuck in that situation, this memory created a trauma around being trapped. Going through this trauma discovery and healing process in therapy was really interesting because I've always hated being tickled. I've wet myself numerous times throughout my life when being tickled, and I didn't know why. Now it all makes sense.

Like I said, initially, I thought I had experienced abuse, but then I opened my eyes and realised that I was just being tickled. As a three-year-old, I felt trapped. I was embarrassed and ashamed, and I didn't know how to deal with those feelings. Those feelings of being trapped stayed with me well into adulthood and never played out in a healthy way, as you'll see as my story continues.

WORLD-CLASS TANTRUM THROWER

As a kid, I had anger issues. I threw a lot of tantrums, and Mum talks about how I would bite down on something or just throw myself on the ground until I got my way. I would bang my head until it bled, and I would basically throw the 'best' tantrums in the world.

I'm seeing some of this behaviour in my own son now, which is quite confronting. But, with what I've learnt, I'm hoping I can help him manage it better as he grows up. I want to comfort him like I probably would have liked to have been comforted. My parents were great, and I'm not saying they did anything wrong. They did everything they could with the skills they had, but I'm hoping I can manage my son's emotions and reactions in a different way. It's a completely different world we live in now, and we understand that the environment outside of the family home plays a bigger role than we once thought. It's why I won't sit back and blame anyone, but I will take responsibility for everything moving forward.

THE DEVIL IS IN THE DETAILS (FREQUENT NIGHTMARES)

Mum told me recently that from the age of six, I thought I was possessed by the devil.

We lived in Murrumbeena until I was around five, and then we moved to Mooroolbark. It was a pretty big move for me as a young kid. Even as a five-year-old, I remember feeling anxious about leaving Murrumbeena. It felt like such a big deal to move away from my friends and my school. Even though it all went well and I fit into my new school, those feelings of anxiety stayed with me and continued to affect me.

From around the age of six, I've had nightmares. They still happen now, but they're much less frequent. When I was a child, I'd have these nightmares so frequently, often nightly. When I started having the nightmares, they were about me being chased around the house by a devil-type creature. I remember them so vividly: I would be chased out of my bed, through the back door of the house, around the house, and up to the garage.

Knowing I would experience these nightmares over and over, going to sleep was really difficult. Because I didn't sleep well, I was always tired. Most of the time, I didn't want to sleep, but I didn't want to wake up either. The nightmares were terrifying because they felt so real to me, and I couldn't escape them.

SPORTING MY WAY THROUGH SCHOOL

One of the happiest parts of my childhood was sport. I was always quite good at each level I played at. I wasn't going to state level or anything like that, but I was always good in my local and school teams.

I was popular in school, and it sounds silly looking back now, but I always had 'girlfriends' in primary school. I had a good group of friends, who loved me and treated me like everyone else. As you'll discover, this isn't how it felt all the time, but hindsight shows me the true value in the people who walked beside me at my lowest moments.

I was also quite popular through high school because I had my footy friends and my cricket friends. Outwardly, I had no logical reason to feel down on myself. But the brain doesn't always act logically, does it?

CHASING CHILDHOOD DREAMS

When I was a kid, I had two dreams for my life. One, I wanted to be a stay-at-home dad. I've wanted this since a really young age. Unfortunately, this can't be a reality for most fathers, as someone's got to earn money, but life has a funny way of working out.

Two, I wanted to be an actor. Right from a young age, I really wanted to be on *Neighbours*. Maybe this was because I used to watch it with Mum all the time, but I loved acting and drama. Looking back, my love for acting came from a place of not wanting to be the person I was. When I was acting, I wasn't me; I was someone else. From a young age, the idea was to always run away from who I was, what I was thinking, and how I was feeling, but, no surprise, running away never worked.

CHAPTER 3

EARLY TEENAGE YEARS AND WANTING TO DIE

NO ONE SHOULD EVER HAVE TO FEEL LIKE THIS

"Why do you do this?" is a question that comes up quite often in reference to me being completely open about my mental health struggles. A lot of things do come to mind in response, but it keeps coming back to this as my number one factor: I don't want anyone to feel like I did when I was 13, lying under my bed, crying, and wanting to be dead.

That feeling and those thoughts, which were extremely painful over years and years, broke me down. I don't want anyone to feel that deep pain, the lack of self-worth, the self-hatred, or the complete loneliness… not the loneliness of being alone but of being in a room full of hundreds of people and still feeling completely lonely.

Then there's the feeling that you aren't meant to be here. It all sucks, and none of it's true, but the feelings and thoughts take over. I don't want anyone to feel any of those feelings if I can prevent it. That's why I do what I do with Power, Strength & Vulnerability (PSV). I want every single human to feel like they are somebody, because every human deserves that.

A BORN LEADER

In primary school, I became a leader. I was house captain for two years in a row, a position that was voted on by my peers. In the voting process, I had to present my case for why I'd be a good house captain, and I was very sporty and social, so this seemed simple to me. In under twelves cricket too, we had to vote for the captain. There were 14 of us in the team, and 13 voted for me (including myself).

Clearly, I fell into leadership positions in sport from an early age. I could always just get into a sporting group and talk and help people, and that was something I was really proud of. However, at the same time, sport was probably one of my triggers as well. A few times, I punched the ground out of frustration or anger, overreacting to certain situations, even at a young age.

However, sport was always my outlet, a space to get away from feelings of self-hatred and the pain associated with thoughts of suicide. So, when things got too much at my 'outlet', I'd explode, and I'd punch the ground, a tree, or a wall because I thought I deserved to be in pain. Any injury I sustained was then a constant reminder for weeks or months that I'd failed again. Well, I thought I'd failed, but, in reality, I just didn't know how to regulate my emotions, and the daily pain I felt would all come out in one massive outburst, like a volcano erupting.

FAILURE TO MANAGE INSUBORDINATE EMOTIONS

When I was a kid, I didn't have the management skills to express my emotions. As I have learnt more about managing emotions and mental health, this has become more and more obvious to me. I'm no expert in it yet, and I'm still learning, for the sake of myself, my children, and the people around me. I'm learning to express my emotions in a healthy way, not in an unhealthy way that causes damage, and I want to model this for others and allow them to do it in a way that feels safe and secure to them.

My struggles with punching things, I'll be honest – it only stopped a couple of years ago. However, for many years, it still occurred a couple of times a year when something really frustrated or upset me. I would *never* punch someone else because I never wanted to hurt anyone else. Doing so would only make me feel worse, so I'd always punch the ground, a wall, a tree, something like that.

It's safe to say that my hands are pretty stuffed. I think I've broken each of my hands twice and potentially my wrists on other occasions too. I didn't get them checked because I thought, *You did it, so you can put up with it*. Throughout high school, I got pretty good at writing with my non-dominant hand.

In my twenties and early thirties, my fallback was still to suppress my suicidal thoughts and hide my feelings. So, when mates threw some banter out or had a joke, I would get triggered and react poorly. I've come to understand that my response is completely my responsibility. My reactions – my *over*reactions – were among the things I needed to work on for myself and everyone around me.

TRAPPED IN A MENTAL PRISON

Those high school expressions of anger were when it started to become a lot realer for me. As well as intense emotions and feeling trapped, the lack of understanding and knowledge about mental health compounded everything. I now know I had anxiety and depression but back then, I didn't even know what those words meant.

This is one of the big reasons why I'm now a huge fan of and advocate for the work Matt Runnalls does with Mindfull Aus. The program 'Healthier Hearts & Lighter Minds' is something I believe would've helped me throughout school and in life.

BULLYING TO BE 'ONE OF THE BOYS'

In school, I experienced a bit of bullying from a few of the older kids. One of these people is a friend today, and, one day, he sat me down and apologised. Back then, it was something we did to each other to be 'one of the boys', but he didn't realise how it might have affected me. I kind of brushed it off at the time, but I know it affected me more than I led on… I felt I deserved it.

In primary school, I was like that as well, bullying other kids. I didn't realise my behaviour was wrong, and I'd give a couple of kids shit because I thought they could take it. We all pretended to be tough, but, looking back, none of us would have taken it well. It was kids being kids, but I'm glad that I learnt to treat people in more healthy and positive ways and that I can model that to my kids today.

I was definitely not bullied to the extent that other kids were, but it probably added a bit of a bitter cherry on top to the way I already felt about myself.

Fortunately, I did have good friendship circles, so the instances of bullying were few and far between. But I do remember that in year eight, a couple of kids from year ten threw me around a bit. As my head was thrown into a locker and I was then thrown into a fence, part of me felt that I deserved it. It was a punishment for being different. At the time, I laughed it off with mates, but I was scared, and it triggered some deep suicidal thoughts and plans.

The reason for the bullying – a girl. What I know now is that bullying quite often comes from our own insecurities, so I'm able to look back with care, empathy, and understanding for all involved. While the pain felt deeper each time I was bullied, I was already in a bad place mentally, so it only further enhanced the belief that everyone would be better off if I was dead.

WHEN SUICIDAL THOUGHTS INVADED MY LIFE

My suicidal thoughts started at the beginning of high school, when I was 13 years old. I didn't know where the thoughts came from or why I was having them. I just knew I didn't want to be here anymore.

I wasn't seeing the attitude or behaviour I was exhibiting modelled anywhere outside of my own head. It wasn't on the TV shows I watched or on the social media I used. So, as far as I knew, the urge to kill myself came from within. For me, those thoughts just emerged.

I know now that they probably stemmed from months upon months of fear, anxiety, and a compounding lack of self-worth and self-esteem. I genuinely thought that everyone around me hated me. I thought they would be better off if I wasn't on this planet anymore. I thought my family, my friends, everyone would be better off without me.

Of course, these thoughts were totally irrational. My family loved me, and my friends enjoyed spending time with me. I was doing well in school, getting picked for sports, and had no trouble finding girlfriends. On paper, I had no reason to be feeling the way I did – but it didn't matter. My thoughts weren't based on reality; they came from within. They were anxiety-fuelled misconceptions, and they completely took over.

Throughout the first few years of high school, I had one friend who I could rely on when my thoughts overwhelmed me. Often, at the end of the school day, I would walk home, go straight to my bedroom, and crawl under my bed. From there, in the dim light, I would text my friend, telling her I wanted to kill myself. It was a lot to put on a teenage girl, who was going through her own shit, but I didn't know where else to turn. Because I lacked the knowledge to manage myself, I relied on her a lot. Ideally, I should have reached out to a professional, someone who really could have helped, but I didn't know that was an option. I didn't know I had alternatives. So, at the beginning of high school, my friend was the only support I had. She was the only person who was aware of what I was feeling and experiencing.

I hid my mental health struggles well from my family. My younger brother, Steven, was in primary school at the time and would arrive home about 40 minutes after me. If I was in my room, hiding from

> ## Lifesaver #1 – Grace
>
> Thank you...
>
> In the moments when I was grappling with how I would take my own life, you accepted my phone calls, returned my texts, and showed an open heart, giving me a space where I could get some of the things trapped in my head out into the world.
>
> We were only 13 years old, but I knew then that you were saving me from doing something that could be harmful.
>
> Our friendship was tested at times, but you stood up when I needed you most, and I'm forever grateful.
>
> Everyone needs a Grace at some stage during their mental illness journey.

the world, as soon as I heard the front door open, I would shoot out from under the bed and walk out like everything was fine.

Eventually, however, the pressure would build up to critical levels, and I would erupt in a volcanic outburst. I would fly off the handle completely, usually punching something for good measure. The pressure could take weeks or even months to build but once I reached the point where I was ready to erupt, even the smallest thing could set me off.

Of course, people would try to reason with me.

"Calm down."

"It's not that big of a deal."

"You're overreacting."

What they didn't know about, what they couldn't see, was the intense self-hatred I was constantly carrying around with me. All of those negative emotions were hidden in my room, under my bed, deep inside me. Whenever I erupted, most people thought I was overreacting. Some thought I was looking for attention. None understood the truth.

Gradually, angry outbursts turned into running away. When I lost control, I would leave people's houses, leave parties, leave friends, leave friendships. Do you remember the Craig David song, 'Walking Away'? Well, people often played that song when I was around. I was the guy who walked away whenever a situation got too tough to handle. I did see the funny side of the joke, but there was also a dark side. Those sudden desertions that inspired my mates to associate me with that song had been months in the making. To me, it wasn't a joke.

Fundamentally, I didn't know how to verbalise what was going on inside my head, so I didn't try.

I'm going to fail at school.

I'm not actually good at sport.

People don't like me.

I'm going to kill myself.

My family is better off without me.

My self-esteem was practically non-existent, and my thoughts reflected this. I didn't understand what was happening at the time;

I didn't know how to analyse and address it. I was just reacting. It was about this time that the nightmares evolved.

My nightmares went from me being chased and possessed by the devil to making realistic attempts to kill myself. In my dreams, I would attempt suicide in many different ways, and every attempt ended the same. Picture a road with a big opening in the middle, like a manhole, something the ninja turtles would jump down to go underground. I'd pop up from there after the attempt to take my life, and there would be a ring of people a full 360 degrees around me. Every face I saw was lifelike and familiar. They were my friends and my family, echoing, "You can't even do this right."

For these reasons, I never wanted to go to sleep. And when I woke up, I didn't want to get out of bed. I didn't want to go to school. I didn't want to see my friends. I didn't want to do anything. Every night for around five years, this was my life.

The only time I got any relief was on the nights before I played sport. Sport was my outlet, and it helped repress the dreams and the suicidal thoughts. It was my only distraction from everything that was going on inside my head, which shows how debilitating and exhausting this illness can be.

CHAPTER 4

LATE TEENAGE YEARS – THE STRUGGLE INTENSIFIES

SCHOOL JUST GOT IN THE WAY

While battling my mental health issues, I struggled with school as well. I'm really academic in my own way, but I struggled with how school was taught. I don't read and retain information; I learn by doing things. I still did pretty well academically for most of school but by year ten, it just got too much for me. I was really good at health and maths subjects, but I didn't do well in English (but here I am writing a book – go figure).

There was also this fear of being smart and not being accepted by the cool kids at school. I felt trapped, not because I didn't want people to like me but because I already thought people didn't like me. I think that's a misconception about the anxiety around people not liking you. It's not that I was trying to be liked; it was that I was trying not to be more disliked. I already thought I was disliked, and I didn't want to make it worse, so I focused on seeming 'fun' to the people around me and not letting school get in the way of that.

One thing I did in school was ignore the 'not so cool' kids, but, to me, that never felt right. I thought I needed to be cooler myself, which is probably why I acted the way I did. Some of those people, I'm now friends with. Not only did ignoring the not so cool kids not make me cooler, but I likely missed out on some great friendships too.

SCREAMING FOR SUPPORT

When you're a teenager who doesn't know how to express your emotions, you feel like your peers and the people around you don't understand everything you're going through – even if they might be going through the same things on the inside. Life looked so good on the outside, but I still felt awful inside. On top of my suicidal thoughts and mental health struggles, my nightmares meant I never slept through the night because I was being tormented by my own brain. It was so hard to function in my life, and it felt like it was all out of my control. The feeling of my own brain being out of my control was torturous.

My mates wouldn't have had a clue about what was going on with me internally. They saw the outbursts, me running away, trying to contain my emotions and not being able to, but they wouldn't have been able to help or understand in any way. I think if I had tried to talk to them about my mental health, it would have been brushed aside. They would have said, "Hey, look around you, you shouldn't feel bad." But I knew what was around me, and it didn't help. It was about what was within me – and it still is. The words of my family and people who were telling me I was being unreasonable or overreacting would have been reinforced tenfold if I had confided in my friends. I'm certain my mental health struggles would have been dismissed or misunderstood. This was more a sign of the times than anything, and I'm sure I would have thought and acted the same in their position.

It was so frustrating because on top of what I was already experiencing, feeling like I had to hide what was going on made it even worse. When I hid under my bed, I desperately wanted to escape what was going on in my mind, and then I'd have to come out and put a mask on for everyone around me. I had to pretend that I was happy and cool and that everything was fine. It was so fatiguing, and bottling it all up was what led to my suicide attempt.

SOCIETY'S SUICIDE STIGMA

There were many situations throughout my teenage years that reinforced the idea that suicide was a weakness and what people with mental health struggles, including myself, were going through was irrelevant.

One day, in early high school, my entire class was brought into our form room, and we were advised that one of the year 12 students had taken his own life. I knew of him because he played at my footy club, and my best friend's older brother was best friends with this guy. My best mate and I had grown up together since we were five. We had played football and cricket together, and his older brother and best friend had always been around at the same sports clubs and games. My best friend and his older brother are great, but, like most teenagers, they lacked understanding around the issues of suicide and mental health.

I remember seeing how much it broke the community around this year 12 boy. That weekend, the whole under eighteens team went and made a circle on the footy ground to pay tribute. This guy was probably one of the most liked people in that year level, and it was a really popular year level of kids – so many people at my school knew the kids in that year. You don't often know many people four years older than you at high school, but I knew so many

LATE TEENAGE YEARS – THE STRUGGLE INTENSIFIES

of that year through sport. They were a big group of friends, and I remember how much it affected them.

There was a girl in my form room class whose boyfriend was in that year level. On the morning when we were told about this kid taking his own life, we walked outside of the form room, and she said, "I can't believe someone would do that. How fucking selfish of him." Instantly, I thought, *Yep, I can never speak about this. I can never talk about how I'm feeling. I can never talk about my suicidal thoughts.*

How could I tell someone I was having suicidal thoughts when that was the standard reaction? They weren't thinking about how much pain that guy was in; they were just thinking about themselves as the people left behind.

My brain took this and ran with it. Instead of thinking, *Maybe this is the pain that other people will be in if I do it,* I thought, *Maybe they don't care. Maybe they don't care about me, and it's all about them. Maybe suicide is actually the best thing.* When these feelings arose, I tried my best to shut them down.

The same scenario played out on three separate occasions during year seven and eight, with our form room teacher keeping us back late to deliver a message. A message delivered to all form rooms throughout the school. A message about a fellow student taking their own life through suicide.

There weren't any details, and the word suicide didn't always get mentioned. But we all knew exactly what had happened: a young male, a brother, a son, a mate, a boyfriend had just ended his life because of the pain he felt inside. He believed that the world and the people in it were better off without him, but this belief is never true.

Such tragedies create a ripple effect of pain and questions. Friends with questions. Family with questions. Strangers with questions. Everyone has questions, but no one has any answers. Why? Because no one expects this to happen.

"No one could've seen this coming," they say. "It's so out of character."

Each one of those mornings, learning that a fellow student had taken his own life, left me feeling numb and lost. People always reacted the same:

"How could he do this?"

"What a selfish thing to do."

"Why would he do this to his family?"

The more I witnessed these reactions, the more I bottled up my own thoughts and feelings. I thought I was crazy, weird, different, and my thoughts and feelings weren't worthy of discussion. In my mind, I couldn't be helped. I knew nothing about mental illness. I didn't even know it was a thing. I feared the judgement of my friends and family for the feelings, emotions, and thoughts I had. This wasn't the only reason why I never spoke up, but it was a huge factor. How could I bring myself to explain what was going on inside my own head when I saw how people reacted to suicide? Yep, the stigma was real.

Thankfully, we've come a long way since then. Knowledge is being passed around in schools, and the stigma has been reduced.

LATE TEENAGE YEARS – THE STRUGGLE INTENSIFIES

The kids I've had the pleasure to present my story to are filled with questions and want to know how to help themselves and others. It's amazing to see.

Unfortunately, however, suicide deaths are still too high. Really, any number is too high. As a community, we need to work together to improve mental health for all. It's not just a problem for those who suffer from mental illness. It's a joint fight forward. If we're ever going to make a real impact, we need to work together. Period.

As sufferers, we need to know that some people won't understand what we're going through. They won't know how to talk about mental illness or suicide. People have lives, and we can't expect them to be there for us 24/7. On the flip side, non-sufferers need to know how small of an effort is needed to help someone who is suffering. Often, it's the small things that matter most, and some of those small things others did for me will be filtered through this book.

As the years went on, I started speaking up, but something still held me back a lot of the time.

"I'd rather kill myself than…"

How often did you hear this growing up? For me, it was a regular occurrence. I even said it myself, as I wanted to fit in, and I had to put people off the scent. I couldn't have them finding out that I *did* actually want to kill myself from time to time.

Every time I heard that phrase or said it myself, I felt more stigma around speaking up about what I was feeling. People would also joke about jumping off the West Gate Bridge. To some, it was funny. But every time I heard it, I felt sick to my stomach because it made me think about my suicidal thoughts again. It made me think that maybe I was better off doing it.

Ultimately, the problem was mine, not anyone else's. I had to learn to change my mindset because, in this life, people are going to say things that make us uncomfortable. They're going to make jokes; they're going to say things we don't like; sometimes, they're going to act like complete dicks – but it doesn't matter. The only things that matter are how we respond and how we treat ourselves.

So, think before you speak, but also think before you react. Often, people don't understand the effect their words can have.

EVERY WEEKEND WAS THE SAME...

I never attempted suicide in high school. My first attempt was when I was 21. Throughout my early high school years, I was really struggling with my mental health, but I sort of just went about my business. Everything stayed behind closed doors.

It wasn't until I started going to parties in the final years of high school that people finally started seeing a lot more of my mental health issues. My friends saw more of the behaviours that my mental health struggles were driving. I was running away, punching things, disappearing.

I would also send drunk messages to friends. I couldn't tell you how many messages I sent about my depression and suicidal thoughts that really worried people. Now, when I'm struggling and

I react poorly to something, my friends push back and tell me I can't act like that. They put up with that behaviour weekly for over ten years so when they see one singular action or reaction, it's part of the collective for them.

As I said, in late high school, there were no suicidal actions, but I definitely experienced suicidal thoughts, and I told people around me about them in really unproductive ways. Most weekends, I'd be out drinking, and I'd start talking about wanting to kill myself. Every weekend, it was the same thing: I would become suicidal, make my way out of the party or nightclub, and head for home, making no progress and only getting worse.

THE IMPORTANCE OF CONNECTION AND SUPPORT

The other side of this was how the messages, particularly the messages I sent to girls, were received. My friends joked about this at my 21st birthday party, and I understand why.

I would often message girls, asking them to come over and cuddle. Everyone always thought it was for sex, but the reality is, I just needed someone with me because I wanted to kill myself. I couldn't come to terms with my emotions, and I needed someone to help me through it. I thought girls could help.

I always felt like I couldn't talk to guys about my struggles because we didn't talk about that stuff. In my mind, they wouldn't understand, and I feared being laughed at, but I felt like I could open up to girls. With that said, the way I opened up to women was completely unhealthy. I pushed everything onto them, which was way too much.

So, when I messaged girls at 3 am, it wasn't for sex. Even if something sexual did eventuate, I'd often wake up afterwards, and go, *Why the fuck did I do that?* I felt so much regret and guilt, and it had nothing to do with the girls and wasn't personal, but sex just wasn't what I wanted. I wanted comfort and safety and connection, and I didn't know how to get those things. I didn't feel like I could get them from male friends. I thought that if I tried to talk to the guys I was friends with, their solution would have been drinking until the sun came up to forget.

There was one girl who I was friends with during that period of time, and her boyfriend and his friends thought I was interested in her, but that was so far from the truth. She was the friend who was there for me. She was the one who would come over at 3 am because I needed help. Quite often, in the middle of winter, we'd sit down on my driveway and talk. I don't like seeing other people suffer, but she'd be freezing while we sat there for hours, and I wouldn't even offer my jumper because that was the headspace I was in. I'm not proud of that, but I had no awareness of anyone else around me, aside from thinking they didn't like me.

This friend helping me probably happened less than I think it did, but I feel like it happened heaps because of the impact she had on me. There were multiple times when she answered my call or message and insisted on coming over to help me and be with me.

LATE TEENAGE YEARS – THE STRUGGLE INTENSIFIES

> ## Lifesaver #2 – Elyce
>
> My teenage years were when my suicidal tendencies were at their most rapid... weekly and, at worst, daily from the ages of 13 right up until 21.
>
> Firstly, I know it wasn't fair for a lot of this to be dumped on you but if I hadn't been able to speak up like I could when I was with you, I simply wouldn't be here today.
>
> It's hard to find the words when you know someone genuinely saved your life... You turned up at the perfect time, were respectful, and gave me the space to verbalise what I needed or to sit in the silence, allowing me to feel safe.
>
> A journey that's so clouded with thoughts of suicide is extremely difficult without the Elyce's of the world. The ones who care, who empathise, who don't make it about themselves, are what we all need.
>
> Thank you.

When she came over, we'd sit and talk for hours. I needed that help and connection to feel safe.

One time, it was 4 am on a summer's morning. A car drove past, and all I could think was, *That person is out to get me.* There was absolutely no reason to think this, but, in my head, it was all I could think.

I was dealing with these suicidal thoughts inside me and when I walked into reality, there was this complete fear and overwhelming feeling of not wanting to be there. While my friend gave me comfort, anything else outside of that didn't. I hope she knows how much she helped me. As we got older, we drifted apart, and she had a lot of other stuff going on in her life – but I hope that she can understand that she 100 percent saved my life. There were times when I was completely blind drunk and out of control when she turned up and talked me through it. If she hadn't been there, I don't know what my family would have walked into. Those are scary thoughts, and I'm glad I got through those times.

THE SCHOOLIES INCIDENT I DON'T LIKE TO DISCUSS

I don't talk about the schoolies incident too often due to the amount of distress it caused others. Recalling the situation hurts because I don't want to see anyone in pain, and, in this case, I was the one causing the pain, which fed into my desire to take my life. So, my suicidal thoughts caused others distress, and their distress fuelled my suicidal thoughts. It was a vicious cycle, for sure.

At the end of high school, I went to schoolies on the Gold Coast with some mates, which, for someone with a poor drinking history, probably wasn't the smartest idea.

One night, after drinking hard throughout the day, I got completely suicidal and ended up messaging a whole bunch of people who were out that night. One particular friend, Steven, ended up saving my life. He was a straight shooter and wasn't going to entertain any of my shit.

LATE TEENAGE YEARS – THE STRUGGLE INTENSIFIES

We were standing on the grass near the hotel when everything came to a head.

"I'm done," I said. "I'm walking straight into the ocean, and I'm not coming back." As I moved towards the beach and the ocean, a sea of inky blackness in the night, Steven tried to talk me out of it. I don't recall what he said; I'm not sure I was even listening. It wouldn't have helped anyway. "Just try and fucking stop me," I said.

And he did.

Steven tackled me right into a bush, where, in my drunken state, I laid for a while before he helped me back up. Despite some resistance from me, he managed to get me back to the hotel room. However, the incident wasn't over.

"I'm going to jump off the balcony," I said.

But Steven wasn't having it.

He managed to keep me in the room – and off the balcony – until the other boys returned. When they came into the hotel room, Steven and I were in one of the bedrooms, door locked, talking. Everyone knew about my meltdown, and one of the boys was furious about the incident. He was trying to break the bedroom door down, yelling for me to 'do it'. "If you're going to jump, fucking jump," he said. I know I had a lot of delusions around people not liking me, but I swear this guy really didn't like me.

The taunting went on for about half an hour, and, during that time, I repeatedly told Steven to let the guy in so he could beat the shit out of me. I just didn't care.

"I can't let him in the room," Steven said. "Because if he does try to beat the shit out of you, you'll just lay there and let it happen." He wasn't wrong.

Lifesaver #3 – Steven (Butcha)

One from the shadows...

It's a night I still sit uncomfortably with but without you, the story would undoubtedly be a different one. You turned up from the shadows with only one task in your head, and that was to stop me from acting on my messages.

Growing up, I didn't think you'd ever need to save me but despite you being the ultimate comedian, you were also the ultimate mate. You have a heart of gold and just thrive on human connection.

Truthfully, that night was the night when it was all going to end.

I sit back, and I have no doubt that without you in that moment, standing by my side, I wouldn't be here thanking you today.

The role you played is one so many play out every day. It's a hero role, and *you* played the superhero for me that night.

Thank you for being my lifesaver.

Eventually, the situation fizzled out, and the night came to an end.

Even though I'd had who knows how much to drink, my memories of that night are so vivid, so clear, so real. Memories like that, they never leave you. No, they follow you around for the rest of your life.

SUICIDAL THOUGHTS TAKE A TURN FOR THE WORSE

It wasn't until I started drinking that my suicidal thoughts morphed into suicidal ideation. What I mean is that I started to plan how I would do it.

One night when I was 20 years old, I stormed out of a nightclub in Ringwood, purposely bumping into the bouncer on the way out.

"Watch it, mate," the bouncer said.

I stopped and faced him. "I don't care what you do," I said. "I'm going to jump in front of a car anyway."

"Go do it then."

That was all the encouragement I needed.

Before I explain what I did next, I should probably add some context. Why was I storming out of a nightclub with suicide on my mind? Well, a girl had slapped me for texting her sister. To this day, I don't know what the problem was. The girl I was texting was a couple of years younger than me, which might have been what triggered the incident, but there was nothing untoward going on. Of course, my confusion around the incident only fuelled my belief that no one liked me and I was better off dead. *I need to kill myself,* I instinctively thought as I stormed out of the club.

At that point, I genuinely didn't care what happened to me, which is why I tried to pick a fight with a bouncer who was practically twice my size and could have beaten me to a pulp if he wanted to. When someone doesn't care what happens to them, it stems from a complete lack of self-worth. I understand that now. But the bouncer didn't need to lift a finger to hurt me because I was determined to do the job myself.

At two o'clock in the morning, I ran out onto the Maroondah Highway and into oncoming traffic. Cars swerved; drivers beeped their horns, and tyres screeched. People hurled abuse at me from their vehicles, which only reinforced the idea that I deserved to die. At that time of morning, the lighting wasn't great, and I was shocked that no one hit me. But I survived the night and eventually made my way home, living to see another day.

When you're in that 'I don't care' mindset, risky behaviour is a part of the package. As far as I know, my friends were unaware of what I did when I left the club. But if they'd seen me running up and down the highway, they would have known that something was seriously wrong. At that time, however, I was alone, and the only witnesses were the pissed off people in their cars.

In these situations, I never wanted to hurt anyone else. I didn't want anyone else involved. But on that night, I lost control, and I put everyone on the highway at risk, not just myself. If someone had hit me with their car, it wouldn't have just hurt or killed me, but it would have changed their life as well. Really, it was a selfish and thoughtless thing to do.

THE PERFORMANCE I RUINED (ANXIETY, GUILT, SHAME)

Let's go back to school. Specifically, year 12. That's when what I now know as anxiety really started to screw with me.

Growing up, I always wanted to be an actor. In order to get into acting school, I knew I had to do well in my theatre studies and my performances. At one point during the year, I was supposed to participate in a group performance. So, I learnt all my lines and prepared as much as I could. The performance was a big deal, and I had a lot riding on it. My entire future as an actor was at stake. At least, that's what I believed.

On the day of the performance, the pressure was too much, so I messaged my drama teacher and said I couldn't do it. By then, I think my teachers knew I was suffering mentally, and they never pushed me too hard. I'd been rebelling in school quite a bit, defiantly wearing my white Globe skate shoes, which I thought made me look like the coolest kid in school. Whenever I got detention, I simply didn't attend, and I never met any real consequences. I can't say for certain, but I suspect the teachers collectively decided to go easy on me. They never fully enforced the rules with me, and I got away with a lot.

Anyway, they gave my role to someone else, and I attended the performance as a spectator – which was a big mistake. The guy who took my part didn't know his lines, which was fair considering the last-minute switch, so he had to read from a script. If you've ever seen a stage show where an actor has to read their lines during the performance, you'll understand how bad it was. I was gutted. The show was ruined, and it was all my fault.

I ran home, turned off my phone, and locked myself in my bedroom cupboard. Anxiety turned to guilt, which turned to depression, which swiftly turned to the urge to kill myself. I sat there in the dark until my brother got home from school. When I heard the front door open, I composed myself, left the cupboard, and walked out of my room like nothing had happened. As usual, I couldn't let anyone know what I was feeling, what I was thinking. In my mind, they wouldn't understand.

I now know that I experienced a complete anxiety attack. At the time, I didn't understand it. I didn't know what was happening. I just knew that I was overwhelmed with guilt and shame. By pulling out of the performance, I'd let everyone down and jeopardised my chances of becoming an actor. I'd managed to both ruin the performance and my life at the same time. *Well done, Shane. You've done it again.* At that point, my life didn't feel like it was worth living.

ANXIETY DOESN'T STICK TO A SCHEDULE

Anxiety can hit at weird times. Sometimes, when the alarm goes off at 8 am, my stomach feels like there's a knot tied in it, and my heart's racing, creating a pain in my chest.

I know this feeling is anxiety, but it doesn't stop the panic in me. My head tells me what it is, but my body doesn't allow a positive change. The negativity and anxiety just keep coming as I begin to sweat.

I grab my phone to distract myself from what's happening with my body as my breath gets shorter and shorter. It doesn't work, so I try to get myself back to sleep, but, as I close my eyes, the irrational thoughts come through and take over my mind. Sleep is impossible.

This happened once when I was about to start a new job, but, at the time, I didn't realise. I'd woken up, anxious and panicking. After five minutes, which felt like an hour, it clicked for me. I was starting a new job in four hours, and I was having a panic attack about it.

The new job was coaching football for a year four school class at an international school. How scary could it really be, letting kids just run around, kicking and handballing? Well, the mind can play its own games, handballing anxious thoughts around: *What if I fail? What if the kids laugh at me? What if I stuff something up in a demonstration? What if, what if, what if?* These thoughts just wouldn't stop, and, in my panicked state, I thought about calling in sick.

I was looking forward to the job. I was super excited and had planned the whole first session, but the morning panic attack still happened due to the fear of trying something new. Anxiety completely took over my body, and the next four hours getting ready and getting to work were a complete blur. When I arrived, the nerves and anxiety were still there, but, somehow, I managed to contain the voices in my head telling me to drive back home. I didn't know what I was walking into, and the fear of the unknown made me expect the worst.

On reflection, the session was a bit of a nightmare, but that just meant I had plenty to learn and work on – which was great. Halfway through the lesson, I felt like I was in over my head, and I wanted to just walk away. On my drive home, I thought about quitting because of the way the first day went. *How could I put myself through that again?* However, I pushed through this anxiety and decided to commit to it for at least a week before I made a final decision – and the next week was fantastic. I loved it, despite the occasional tough moment.

Anxiety can be so incapacitating, and, plenty of times throughout my life, I've pulled out of events, work shifts, or social plans because of my anxiety. However, I've learnt from every single experience, which now enables me to work my way through the thoughts in my head and the experiences of my body.

You can do this too – be kind to yourself in those moments and use the skills and techniques you learn along the way to help yourself get through them. Most of all, be super proud of yourself for working through it all.

MY FAMILY LEARNS THE TRUTH

During year 12, I left school for two weeks to work at Hungry Jacks. When I realised I probably wouldn't make it as an actor, my dream was to manage a Hungry Jacks restaurant. Yep, I was thinking big. However, that dream was short-lived, and I quickly returned to school. As it turned out, working at a fast-food restaurant wasn't as glamorous as I thought it would be. It wasn't my passion; it wasn't my dream. If it's yours, I have nothing but respect, but it wasn't for me.

By this time, Mum and my brother had become somewhat aware of what I was going through and how I'd been behaving. Steven often woke up to messages from my friends asking if I'd made it home safely because I'd said I wanted to kill myself. While people probably thought I was attention seeking, I suspect they sometimes wondered, *What if this is the night he actually does it?* So, by texting Steven and explaining what was happening, my friends were looking out for me in the only way they knew how.

I don't know when my family started to learn the truth but once the cat was out of the bag, there was no putting it back in. Most weekends, I was expressing the desire to take my own life. There was no hiding it anymore. At the same time, no one, including me, knew what to do about it, so, for now, the pain continued.

ANOTHER CHANCE AT MY DREAM

After attempting to take on the fast-food world, I went back to school and spoke to the drama teacher. Through that discussion, I realised I still had a chance to pass year 12 theatre studies and follow my dream of being an actor. Everything was riding on one final performance.

This was a solo performance at the local community centre, and it would dictate my overall mark and determine which acting schools I could apply for. *I'm going to be an actor*, I kept telling myself. I recognised I had a real shot at redemption, a second chance, and I thought I could work through everything I'd experienced previously.

You see, while I had the best of intentions, I also had a complete lack of knowledge around how anxiety works, along with zero tools and strategies to work through it when it arose. Maybe, instead of learning algebra in school, we could've learnt about our mental wellbeing and how to regulate our emotions.

During the last couple of months of school, I did everything I could for that performance, including constant rehearsals, practicing in front of the mirror, *everything*. You better believe I was ready to knock the socks off the judges on the day.

That was until the day arrived…

It was as if I went into autopilot. I turned my phone off, put it under my pillow, and sat in my cupboard, where I stayed for eight hours.

I'd done it again. I'd failed again. I was hopeless. I was lost. I'd proved to myself that I didn't have what it took to achieve any of my dreams. All the pain inside got bottled up because I didn't know what I was experiencing, and I wasn't going to tell people I was 'crazy'.

WALKING INTO THE WORLD BLIND

I left high school with no real-world abilities and very little idea about what the real world was actually like. I thought high school was bad, but the next three years were worse. I had no understanding of financials, careers, anything. I was practically walking out into the world blind. On top of that, I was still struggling with the internal war inside my head. Suicide was constantly on my mind.

Nothing I'd learnt in school helped me navigate the world *or* my mental health issues. I was desperately lacking the knowledge I needed to even survive let alone thrive. I'm really big on the idea that the education system needs to change to have any actual impact on the mental health crisis we're living in. It *must* start there, in our schools.

So, when I left high school, I had no skills for managing life outside of the school walls. Our parents can only teach us so much. They've been through the same education system, and, even with life experience, they have their blind spots. Dad started working after leaving school at age 18 and never stopped. It's all he knows. But the times are always changing, and his reality at 18 wasn't my reality at that age. No, life was different back then, as it will be ten years from now. The education system needs to recognise this and adapt.

For me, sport was the only coping mechanism I had. I would turn up to training an hour early and run laps, not so much because I loved training but because if I didn't get there early, I would end up lying in bed, wanting to kill myself. At the footy club, the cricket club, wherever, I was always the first to arrive and last to leave because I needed that outlet for the pain.

I didn't know what to do with my life, so I went back to work at Hungry Jacks.

CHAPTER 5

MY SUICIDE ATTEMPT

UNDERSTANDING WHY

The first suicide attempt that landed me in hospital occurred at age 21. It was the moment that caused my friends and family to realise I wasn't just talking about killing myself for attention. I really was battling those thoughts and those urges. Even so, they didn't fully understand what I was experiencing. They didn't understand the *why*.

From the outside, it looked like I'd tried to kill myself because of a girl, which was partly true, but it was far from the full picture. In the hospital, a friend, who later came to me about his own anxiety, said to me, "It's just one girl, mate. There are plenty more out there."

He, and others, couldn't grasp the reality of what I was experiencing, and I can see why. It wasn't just one girl – that was just the tip of the iceberg. It was simply the incident that reinforced all the negative thoughts and feelings I'd been battling since high school. One failed relationship didn't suddenly make me want to kill myself. No, this had been eight years in the making.

My friend's reaction highlights the lack of understanding some people have about the pain we carry within. They only see the tip of the iceberg, but there's a whole lot more floating beneath the surface. It's not their fault. We just have a long way to go to educate people about what those of us with severe mental health issues are battling.

IT ALL ADDS UP
(EIGHT YEARS IN THE MAKING)

Over the years, my anxiety built and built. When I was driving to my job at Hungry Jacks, if I got a red signal at this one particular traffic light, I would instantly burst into tears. The light was about ten minutes from the restaurant and if I hit a red, I'd need to pull over and call in sick to work. Then I'd either sit in the car for the duration of my shift or go home and pretend my roster had changed. I didn't want my family to know I'd called in sick. This happened roughly every few weeks. Most days, on the way to work, I'd drive really slowly, trying to avoid getting that red light, but sometimes I just couldn't avoid it.

That's how all-consuming my anxiety was. But I didn't know I had anxiety; I didn't know I had depression. I just thought I was crazy, different, unique. It may sound egotistical to say I thought I was 'unique'. It may sound like I have a high opinion of myself. But I'd been beating myself down for eight years, and my opinion of myself was far from high. In fact, it couldn't have been lower.

I'm not saying my ego didn't come into play. It actually played a big part in my behaviour, as I'd do anything to be liked, which is a dangerous path to go down. So many teenagers, especially boys, long to be liked so much that they take it to the extreme. But the thing is, often by trying too hard to be liked, we end up being liked less. Or, commonly, we're taken advantage of. People start wanting things from you, not because of who you are but because of what you're willing to do in order to earn approval. It's people pleasing to the extreme, and it ultimately harms, not helps, you and your relationships in the long run.

Before my suicide attempt, another incident almost pushed me over the edge. I was driving with some friends in the car, and I missed a 60 km sign for roadworks. The police pulled me over and informed me that I was 30 km over the limit. The usual speed limit was 80 km, so I still would have been over by 10 km, which wouldn't have been so bad, but 30 km over the limit... Well, it meant I'd lose my license.

I was gutted. Once again, I'd fucked up, and the only solution I saw was to take my own life – and I wasn't even drinking at the time. I knew I couldn't be around all my friends that night, so I went across town with one friend, a girl who'd been in the car when I got pulled over.

She may not know this, but she saved me that night. I don't think she understood how deeply the incident affected me, but she knew I needed comfort, and she provided it. She's an amazing person.

Essentially, losing my license cost me my job at Hungry Jacks, which, looking back, was a blessing in disguise. Before I left, I was working a lot of 13-hour days, which isn't something anyone who's suicidal should be doing because they can get burnt out and worsen their situation.

Eventually, I got a job as a landscaper, which wasn't something I thought I'd ever do. But I enjoyed the work, and the following six months or so weren't too bad. I spent the time working, playing sport, and drinking with my mates. Also, I met a girl.

For the first time, I felt a true connection with someone. Was it love? Maybe. It was like nothing I'd ever experienced before. There was no judgement, no ridicule, and I could be open about who I was and what I was going through.

Lifesaver #4 — Taryn

This night was another one of those under the radar nights, because it was really only when I was drinking that I opened up about how I was feeling. Suicidal thoughts didn't just creep up when I was substance affected. They also crept up when I was under the immense pressure of failing myself or my friends again. A lot of my friends and family members won't know about these days or nights because I kept them to myself, but they happened weekly throughout this period of my life, when I'd have to lock myself away for fear of what I might do.

That night, I was at breaking point, and the thoughts that crossed my mind included jumping into the Yarra River and running off to another state, plus many other irrational thoughts.

Having someone who just allowed me some time and space to collect my thoughts and feelings saved my life that night... Taryn you are one of my lifesavers, and I'm extremely grateful for you being there when I felt I had no one.

Unfortunately, she left for Europe to work for six months. Later, I learnt it would be a year. Eventually, she broke it to me lightly that it would actually be two years. *What?!* We tried long distance, but it was difficult to coordinate. She was working; I was working, and the time zones were completely mismatched. It was never going to work.

When she left, I saw a psychologist for the first time, and they put me on medication. At the time, I was working a temporary office job before going back to landscaping. One day, I was sitting in my cubicle, and I literally started banging my head against the wall. I messaged Mum and told her she had to come and get me because I was experiencing side effects from my medication. I'd been open about the meds I was taking, so my employer understood why I had to leave that day, and I managed to pull myself out of the downward spiral.

Later, however, on a Friday night, I was at a mate's place drinking and smoking weed. At one point, I went into the backyard. The negative thoughts were rising within, spiralling around inside my head. I couldn't take it anymore, so I banged my head against a brick wall over and over again, trying to silence the self-hatred. Of course, it didn't work. When I came back inside, my mates asked what had happened. Apparently, I had a big graze on my forehead. I told them I was looking at my phone and hit my head – and they bought it.

Given my history, they probably shouldn't have been so quick to believe me. But accidents do happen, and they couldn't have known I was fighting a battle I was about to lose. I don't for one minute hold anyone responsible for what happened next.

THE SCARIEST 15 MINUTES OF MY LIFE

That night, I stayed at my mate's place, where I slept for a good eight hours. When I woke up, I was done. There's no other way to describe it. I was done with life; I was done with living.

My mate was aware of my issues, as I had opened up to him and his mum previously, so I waited until he hopped in the shower, and I left.

That's it. I'm done. I'm going to kill myself.

I should've known better, but I hopped in my car. In that state of mind, I shouldn't have even considered getting behind the wheel, if not for my own safety, then for the safety of others. I was playing that same risky game I'd played as cars swerved to dodge me on the highway in Ringwood. I wasn't just playing with my life but the lives of others too, which is something I'm completely against.

I tried to find a reason not to do it, but all I found inside was emptiness. I drove for 15 minutes, feeling completely numb.

Is there a reason not to do this? I couldn't find one, so I kept driving. If I had stayed with my mate, given him my keys, and talked about what I was feeling, I wouldn't have ended up where I did. The emptiness, the numbness, it was only temporary. When you're feeling that way, it's the absolute worst time to act or make any serious decisions. If you're feeling like that, you need to find a way to be safe until those feelings pass and you're thinking clearer. Whatever you do, *don't* do what I did.

I didn't have a plan. I didn't know how I was going to do it. I made my decision in a split second. As the pole came into view, I pushed my foot down on the accelerator, and it was over.

When I woke up, the first thing I saw was a young man peering through the driver's side window. I glanced around, trying to figure out what had happened. The passenger side of the vehicle was obliterated. Mangled steel, broken glass – the engine was practically on the passenger seat. Anyone sitting on that side of the vehicle would *not* have survived.

The driver's side door clicked open, and the young man leaned in. "Are you okay?"

As I became more lucid, I recalled what had happened, what I had tried to do. "If this is real life, then no, I'm not okay."

At that, the man broke down right there beside me and my totalled car. He understood everything, and it affected him deeply. I didn't know how I had survived. The pole should have hit the driver's side, but it didn't. Somehow, I'd missed hitting it the way I had attended. Maybe I flinched or lost control at the last second. Perhaps someone was looking out for me. Either way, I was alive, which meant I'd failed.

I can't even do this right.

At the time, that was my genuine reaction to surviving a suicide attempt. *I can't even do this right.* I didn't think I was lucky. Nope, not lucky. *Incompetent.* That's what I was. Of course, my attitude has completely changed now. To whatever saved me that day, whether dumb luck or something else, I'm grateful beyond measure. Because I'm here, and I'm okay now. The suffering doesn't need to end the way I tried to end it. There's *always* a better way. I'm glad I realised this when I did because I would have missed out on all the amazing people and opportunities that have come into my life since. *Fuck*, what a terrible mistake I almost made. In the end, I really was lucky, even if I didn't think so at the time.

The young man helped me out of my wrecked car, and we sat and waited for the paramedics to arrive. I don't recall much of what happened next. It's all a bit hazy. At a certain point, I thought, *Shit, now I don't have a car. And I'm probably going to have to pay for the pole.* But I had survived; the numbness was fading, and I was back to living in the real world, with real-world consequences.

Eventually, family members arrived on the scene. They were clearly shocked, but they held it together. More than anything, I think they were just grateful I was alive.

I went to the hospital via ambulance, where I was diagnosed with depression. The doctors changed my medication and from that point on, I was very vocal about mental health and my own struggles. I didn't want to go back to that place again: that empty place where nothing mattered. I *couldn't* go back to that place. I would avoid it at all costs. That period of utter numbness before I tried to kill myself was the scariest 15 minutes of my life. That sense of nothingness was… honestly, only luck could've saved me at that point. That day, I was lucky that luck was on my side. I don't know if anyone could've talked me out of doing what I did. Looking back, I doubt it.

We can't rely on luck to save those who are suffering. Instead, we must be proactive in combating the mental health crisis we're experiencing right now, and the first step to addressing the problem is understanding. The more we understand about what people are going through, the better we'll be able to help them. It's time to take luck out of the equation.

Kind Stranger

The first responder isn't always a police officer or paramedic. It quite often is a member of the public or a family member, and I know what I'm about to write is what a lot of people in my situation wish they could say.

Kind Stranger,

Thank you for being the face, the friendly face. I didn't know what I thought I was meant to see, but I didn't even expect to be alive. I still remember the tears coming down your face, and that's when it hit me that people do care about me. In that hour prior to our meeting, I'd been burdened with the thoughts that no one cared about me and everyone was better off with me dead.

You gave me hope. While my mind was completely muddled, there was still hope.

I'll always be thankful that you were there in my darkest hour, my darkest moment, and I'm so appreciative that I had a non-judgemental, empathetic human there when I opened my eyes.

I haven't met you again since, but I'll never forget that moment in time. While it has been a rollercoaster ride since that moment, the care and compassion you showed plays a huge part in me still being alive and thriving today.

THANK YOU.

I want to say a big thank you to the police and paramedics who attended that day. On top of that, I want to say a big thank you to *all* the first responders who frequently have to deal with these types of situations. I don't know where we'd be without you. Finally, to the guy who arrived first on the scene and helped me out of my car, thanks, mate. I'm sorry you had to see that, but I'm so grateful for your compassion and support. I'll never forget it.

WHAT WAS I GOING TO TELL THE PEOPLE WHO NEEDED TO KNOW?

The days after my suicide attempt are mainly a big blur, with some really vivid memories that stand out.

Fuck… I realised that not only did my family and friends need to know, but I also had a job, and my boss needed to know because I was going to need some time off.

I remember being in the hospital, having to make that call. Would I be fired? My life was about to get a lot harder because I needed a new car and I'd need to pay the council for the pole. How would I manage any of that if I lost my job? My mind was running down the path of wishing I'd succeeded in my attempt, and I hadn't even left hospital yet.

I made the call, and what my boss did shocked me. There were tears on both sides of the phone. My boss was distraught by the news, and I still had a job. He said to take the time I needed before I came back. I was to return to work when I was good to go and no earlier. There was no pressure, which allowed me to just focus on my own wellbeing. Knowing my job was safe was one thing, but it was uplifting to know he cared about me more than money. The human side of me was more important, and I'm forever grateful for his understanding.

That call turned out to be a game changer for me, and I hope other workplaces can offer similar support, because it genuinely helps.

When I went back to work, my boss and another worker, Scott, who was someone I looked up to, provided human support. At different parts of the day, each of them pulled me aside to check in and let me know they were there. Both of them said something along the lines of, "I don't understand, but I'm here to listen," and that's exactly what I needed – honest care and support.

THEY MAY NOT HAVE UNDERSTOOD, BUT THEY LEFT AN IMPACT

By no means was I out of the woods mentally. Eventually, a weekend came around when I was suicidal again, and news of that spread. Someone had called my brother, and, after driving when I shouldn't have, I somehow found my way home. I was embarrassed, ashamed, and full of guilt after all my friends and my football club became aware of suicidal text messages I'd been sending.

Eight days went by, during which time I didn't leave my house, and it was around 9 am on Sunday when a text message came through and anxiety overcame me – sweating, heart racing, hands shaking – as I went to pick up the phone.

"Do you want to go to the footy today?" The message was from Scott from work. As I mentioned, Scott was someone I looked up to, but he was also someone I deeply feared would judge me, and I felt he wouldn't understand at all.

That simple offer to go to the footy made me smile, and, despite declining the offer, I proceeded to leave the house for the first time in eight days. A simple offer changed my world. People didn't need to fix me. I wasn't broken. Connection, support, and love helped me be somewhat whole while *feeling* broken.

CHAPTER 6

THE JOURNEY TO BEING OKAY

HELP, SUPPORT, AND HOPE

While I was in the hospital, I was able to get some space and gain some clarity around psychologists and getting help.

Before my suicide attempt, I'd gone to psychologists, but I'd walked in and sat and talked to them, and walked out thinking, *Great, I'm fine now*, because I felt good. My key message about this is that one session is fucking nothing – you need to really commit and be serious about it. You can go for a year or two or more. It doesn't need to be weekly appointments, but it needs to be consistent and ongoing. If you're really struggling, it may need to be daily or in the hospital, which is what it was for me at one point in my life.

When coming out of the hospital after my suicide attempt and then deciding to get inpatient help several years later, I realised there is such a lack of understanding around mental health and getting help. No one seemed to truly understand why I'd attempted suicide, which made moving forward difficult.

On top of that, I felt guilty that the girl I'd been dating would find out that I'd tried to kill myself and think it was in some way her fault. When she returned to Australia a couple of years later, we tried to rekindle things, but too much trauma had happened in both of our lives, and it didn't work out. However, I was able to tell her that it wasn't her fault. I was really honest with her and said that my suicide attempt had been eight years in the making. I explained that something else would have set me off eventually. I was a ticking time bomb. I reached breaking point and needed a drastic change in my life; I just went the wrong way about making it happen. Hopefully, my story can serve as the breaking point for others so they don't ever reach the point of harming themselves.

In hospital, the most valuable thing I learnt is that when you're at rock bottom, the simple things like getting up and having a shower or brushing your teeth are huge, and we need to do that self-care, even when it feels really hard. It might sound ridiculous but even now when I'm having a great day, I'll still miss a shower or brushing my teeth sometimes. Then I'll pull myself up: *Hang on a minute, I still need to do that self-care.* Self-care is genuinely important for people who are really struggling. We have clients at work who won't shower for weeks, and that's a clear sign that they're mentally unwell. There's no genuine self-care there, and they aren't looking after themselves in the most simple and necessary ways. They also know that if they're not looking after themselves, they'll push people away.

It's a really important thing that I try to be conscious of. It's small, but it's essential. To get me through my lowest of lows, I need to get up, have a shower, have breakfast, and brush my teeth. Then I work with whatever happens after. As I get better at managing these small tasks, my expectations get higher.

What we all need to understand is that when we're not doing well mentally, we have to go back to the basics and know that's okay. Rather than forcing ourselves to do the big things that we don't have the capacity for, it's okay to lower our expectations to what's realistic at that time.

We need to be conscious of this in other people too. People will assume that because I've come so far, now I'm fine, and I shouldn't struggle with things as much. But I still battle at times. After 25 years of conditioning, when some things come up, I can't manage. I get into fight or flight mode. I'm coping and surviving but not managing.

The current stage of my life started when I got serious about getting help and managing my expectations of myself.

WALKING BACK INTO SPORTING CLUBS

Word had spread over the weeks, and I returned to footy training as a spectator. Sitting on the sidelines, watching the boys train, was extremely difficult. Although I probably wasn't able to train physically, it was the mental pain that really kept me off the track.

Negative thoughts continued to rattle through my head, and I sat there thinking I deserved it still.

Why are the boys laughing at me?

They must think I'm crazy.

He's a soft cock – that's what they're thinking.

Sitting there was horrible until Noons, a member of the senior committee, grabbed my attention and broke my irrational thought patterns. "Hey, Kelts…"

My thoughts turned to, *Will they ask me to leave the club?* and, *How much trouble am I in?*, which, on reflection, shows how much work I still had to do on my mental health.

I don't remember word for word what was said, but it was along the lines of, "Kelts, we got together as a senior committee after we heard the news. We were shocked, and on behalf of the committee and the club, if there's anything we can do, please reach out. You're much loved, and we want you around."

I don't have a clue what else was said in that conversation, but those words stuck with me because I realised how important sporting clubs were going to continue to be for me. Every sporting club I've been to since has embraced the true me and accepted my flaws and my vulnerabilities.

When the session was done and the players started leaving the track, I thought I was going to be ignored. Maybe it was what I wanted because of the shame and guilt I still carried. As the first player started to walk over to me, I felt my body temperature rise, and, as I trembled, I met his hand. With a shake of the hand, a simple, "Love ya, Kelts" came out of his mouth before he headed in to get changed.

Over the next 10 to 15 minutes, many other players approached me in the same way, reaffirming how important the communities within sporting clubs were going to be for me moving forward. Some players shared their own experiences with anxiety, depression, and suicidal tendencies. It blew my mind open to the fact that I wasn't alone on this journey, and a feeling of relief overtook my body each time I heard a story.

Something stood out in the stories of those players, who all had great jobs, families, and supportive friends (much like me). I noticed that each story contained a similar thread: no one had told their partners or their families what they were going through.

This common thread left me confused, despite me understanding they didn't want to burden their loved ones. For me, the theme of males between 15 and 35 not speaking up was, and still is, a huge catalyst for me sharing, educating, and giving hope so we can continue to save those who are in the grips of mental illness.

I share the motto 'speak up, speak out' on the clothing I create in hope that it prompts people to speak up when they're suffering and need help.

DIAGNOSIS – MAKING SENSE OF THE SENSELESS

I was so relieved to get my diagnosis. I didn't think I was crazy anymore. All these things that I'd been telling myself for years that I believed to be true – that I was alone, weird, different, the only one – didn't necessarily change, but I had a new outlook and new beliefs. I finally had something to help me make sense of what I was experiencing.

Unfortunately, a few years after that, I got completely stuck in my diagnosis. So, while it was really beneficial, there were also points where it wasn't helpful. What I've learnt is that there's a version of you that's depressed, but having that diagnosis doesn't mean that's you for the rest of your life.

When I got stuck in my diagnosis, I relapsed completely because it became who I was – but it's not who I am. I'm so much more than my depression.

The next few years were a rollercoaster, and, at around age 23, I started writing a lot.

HOW PEOPLE HELPED ME, HOW I MANAGE MYSELF

In the end, the onus was on me to make the changes I needed to make to live a happy and healthy life, but that's hard to come to grips with when it's much easier to ask someone else for the answers and rely on them. Thanks to Nick at MyndFit, I follow one golden rule now: I'm responsible for my health and happiness. With that said, it doesn't mean people can't play a role in supporting us along the way.

The rollercoaster of my teens and twenties was littered with a lot of things people did that helped and a lot of things people did that didn't help. Here, I'm going to focus on a few things that did help, and I hope they're things you can do for someone too. I mentioned support, love, and connection earlier, and they're the key elements to each of the following examples.

As you'll learn later, my mum played a significant role in my journey, and, at times, we had a very heated relationship, one where she would care for me and I would lash out verbally, run away, and, in many circumstances, harm myself because of how I'd treated her. Throughout that period, one of the huge things she did was keep her door ajar for me so, when I was ready, I could go in and speak to her. Eventually, I did start doing that, and sometimes it helped. Quite often, when I was suicidal, scared, and wanting to run away, I'd ask Mum to sit in another room of the house to keep me accountable so I couldn't leave. *But* she wasn't to talk, and I wasn't to see her. If I did see her, I knew I'd be triggered, so I explained the situation, and she became a person who ultimately kept me safe without judgement.

Suicide survivors and those of us who frequently fight dark battles with our own minds always have something or someone that really drives us along and keeps us going. My mum saved me on a regular basis.

Essentially, mates were the most challenging but also the most important people in my life. During that time, I genuinely felt like they mattered most, so what they said ultimately either triggered or comforted me. My mates showed up at some of the most crucial times. They didn't turn up to fix me; they turned up to sit with me in the trenches of my suicidal thoughts. Every single one of them played a significant role in different ways, which included Daniel turning up as I was walking around the house with a knife and Jason coming over to watch the footy in complete silence.

In each of those moments, some key things they did kept me safe:

- They listened with respect and without judgement.
- They gave me physical space when asked.
- They hugged me when I needed it.
- They connected on a human level, focusing on support and love.

What my mates did, which was basically them just being there, made all the difference.

While I was looking after myself and doing what was needed, I was still so heavily focused on the external world, looking for validation, and my internal world wasn't coming to grips with the fact that I needed to be the one doing the work.

From age 25 to 30, I struggled. I relapsed and ended up in hospital. I felt like my own personal lockdown was before COVID even happened because, in 2019, I was already in a bad place.

THE TRICKY BALANCE BETWEEN EXERCISE AND MENTAL HEALTH

Exercise and mental health have had a tricky relationship in my life. In 2016, I was training for an ultramarathon in the Blue Mountains. Back then, my outlet was running. Running was something I knew helped my mental health as well as my physical health, but I got injured. I ended up having two hip surgeries, one in 2016 and another in 2017, and I felt like I lost everything when I lost the ability to exercise for months.

During that time, I basically fell into a hole. So, I had to learn to do other things to manage my mental health. This set me up to win in a way, because you always need balance, but it also set me up to fail, because I tried so many different things, working to find what would help me. It started to wear me out a bit. I was also frustrated because I could see how many other people out there were affected in the same way. They were exercising and when exercise got taken away for whatever reason, they were in a lot of pain.

In 2019, I started to sink further into that hole. The COVID-19 pandemic showed how mentally unwell people can be when they're forced into specific, challenging situations and don't have strategies to deal with them.

I was actually fine through the pandemic. I found connection; I adapted, and I learnt how to deal with it. Before that, I got stuck in my depression because I didn't have the full education, the necessary healing, or the understanding of what was transpiring within me.

For a while, I was living a very bachelor-type life. Even though my childhood dream was to have two kids and be a stay-at-home dad by 25, I was the furthest thing from that. I was going from girlfriend to girlfriend, and I was trying to find connection through having a partner. This is a completely unhealthy way to go about relationships, but a lot of men do it, and it might be too late before they realise it's the wrong approach.

TELLING MY STORY - THERE'S SOMETHING BIGGER AT STAKE

Telling my story has become a part of who I am. I guess because of this, and because I talk about mental health so often, people might read my stuff and think it comes to me so easily. However, there's still a process to this, and it can be difficult.

If I wanted to live a different life, I'd move to the middle of nowhere, get a basic job, and never have to talk about mental health or work on it again. But that's not how this works. I feel like I have to add to this space, and I have to talk about it, because we need help.

Some people reading, watching, or listening to my content might think that's weird, but I have to do this because people will continue to lose their brothers, their best mates, their sons, their dads to suicide if we don't continue to share our stories and make these stories as real as we can. We have to normalise talking about these things because the more we talk about it, the better it gets.

The reality is, I want to do whatever I can and manage whatever happens within me and around me to do that. I say this, knowing that a lot of my friends have drifted away from me because of this and because of the way I can be, which I have to manage. There's something bigger at stake, so I have to do this. I say this unapologetically because people's lives are literally on the line, and I know for a fact I've saved people's lives.

People have come to me and said, "If I didn't read your post, I'd be dead." If I lose some friends because of the work, that's okay because I know we still love each other, but maybe we need distance, and I unapologetically have to accept that. It's brutal, and it's hard, and it's not exactly what I want, but there's a bigger picture.

When I met Alicia, my now wife, I unapologetically said, "This is who I am, and this is who I'll probably continue to be. When I tried to steer away from it, I got more depressed, so I have to do it." So, I can manage backlash, but I can't imagine not being the person who helps and tries to change things. I'm going to continue being authentic about everything and about myself.

SEARCHING FOR MY CALLING, FINDING PERSONAL TRAINING

I started personal training because I was trying to find my calling, and I knew that exercise helped manage my mental health. What I know now is I did need other avenues to help me look after my overall wellbeing, but, at the time, being in the gym, seeing my personal trainer (PT), and running helped me immensely and I knew that if *I* felt the benefits, others would too.

Becoming a personal trainer felt natural to me, and it created a life where I had to practise what I preached. I was helping; I was teaching, and that was something I was extremely proud of. While I'm still working as a PT, I do it so differently now due to the many lessons I learnt through the process.

Lesson #1 – Personal training or going to the gym is not the answer to mental health struggles

Will I cost myself clients by writing this? Maybe, but I've seen so many people who think transforming their bodies and training all the time can help save them or fix their mental health struggles.

Many clients came to me, knowing I'd struggled with my mental health, and I thought I could help them. And I did, but only so much. Earlier, I shared about my poor relationship with running, and it's a trap many fall into. When coaching others and helping myself now, I take a more holistic approach. Physical activity is part of the process for mental wellbeing, but it's not *the* process.

Lesson #2 – Money, money, money

For some personal trainers, money becomes more important than anything else, and, guided by shiny objects, I fell into this trap too. It was the constant money chasing, trying to get and maintain the perfect physique, and trying to help clients do the same that ultimately played a part in my eventual burnout.

So, when coaching now, I focus on the moments and allow the process to be. It takes away the shame and guilt for the individual while helping us understand that we can still try to be better each day. For me, the big lesson here was that I didn't have to always follow the guidance of others if it didn't sit well with me and I was content doing what I was doing.

Lesson #3 – I still believed the negative self-talk

I had many mentors. Each taught me a lot, and I couldn't be more thankful, but the negative self-talk was a constant obstacle I struggled to overcome. The problem wasn't my mentors – they helped as much as they could – but I still had a lot of work to do on myself.

Over the years, a few negative comments about my abilities as a personal trainer were thrown my way, and it was only because I believed them that they affected me. Those comments hit me hard, reinforcing the belief that I would never be a good PT, so I handed over my business to my then girlfriend as I spiralled into the relapse I mentioned previously.

ALL PEOPLE IN ALL INDUSTRIES MUST STAND TOGETHER

A lot of people in the fitness industry are there for the money, and it becomes less work, more profit, which I understand, but that's not true to who I am and what I want to do with my career. As I mentioned, I've been burnt by that kind of money mindset before, and I'm still trying to shake some of those toxic lessons and values I learnt back then.

When I first came into the personal training industry, it seemed like every PT was in it for themselves. It seemed like one big contest. Why though?

We all want one thing, and that's to help people become fitter, stronger, and healthier. We want to help people achieve the dreams they never thought they could. There are enough people who want and need help to go around.

Part of helping people physically is also helping them mentally. I thought we were all on one path with this, but maybe I had my head buried in the sand. The fact is that with mental illness, we must stand together and put our egos aside. If we don't, we'll continually lose people we love, not only to suicide but to life in general. People can become so antisocial that they go 'missing' due to mental health.

If you're in the mental health industry and something is beneficial for people, allow it to happen and get out of the way. Let's work as one to end suicide and keep reducing the stigma around mental illness. We're all human, and we're all on one team.

If we don't stand up now, what *will* it take?

SELF-SABOTAGE MODE ACTIVATED

For so long, I'd been living one way, working in survival mode, just getting by – then my life changed. Suddenly, I was in a serious relationship, which was new to me, and it scared me. Often, it's finally getting the things we really want that are the scariest. My lack of self-esteem and self-worth all came back. I felt that Alicia was too good for me, and all of the anxious and depressed feelings resurfaced. Subconsciously, I did everything in my power to self-sabotage.

Self-sabotage wasn't just an issue in my relationship with Alicia; it was also a problem in my previous relationships. Often, when we suffer from mental health challenges, we form belief systems based on the idea that we don't deserve to be happy, which translates to we don't deserve the *people* or *things* that make us happy. When we're in that frame of mind, we make choices that can ruin our relationships. Whether consciously or unconsciously, we want the other person to end things. Why? Because our belief systems tell us that's what we deserve.

The thing is, it's not just our relationships we tend to sabotage. For me, whenever *anything* started to go well, I would find ways to ruin it. If I was doing well at sports, I would find a way to fuck it up. If I was excelling at a job, I would sabotage myself before I got too successful. If I had money in the bank, I would find ways to blow it. When I left high school, I was making a pretty decent wage. What did I do with that money? I spent it all on other people. I never saved any for myself because, in my mind, I didn't deserve it. Essentially, I did whatever I could to ensure I was always at the bottom of the pile in every aspect of life. I struggled to accept any level of success, and I rarely let a good opportunity go too far.

Remember the school performance I bailed on at the last minute? Moments like that have been a regular occurrence in my life. Often, I'll be right at the end of a big, important project, within spitting distance of the finish line, and I'll put the brakes on at the last minute, undoing months or sometimes years of hard work. When I'm in that frame of mind, failure is the only option.

Consciously, I don't want to ruin my life, but a part of me always wanders down the path of self-sabotage. It may sound counterintuitive but when things are going well, my mental health suffers more than ever. For instance, prior to my suicide attempt, I had the world at my feet. I was succeeding at sport, meeting girls easily, and had plenty of mates. I was on track to set myself up for the future. But I didn't deserve a good future, right? The success became too much, and, mentally, I fell off a cliff. We all know where I landed. When you're wandering through life with that sort of mindset, your relationships are doomed to fail before they begin.

While most of my relationships had 'honeymoon periods', the situation would quickly deteriorate, especially if things were going really well. I didn't deserve happiness, remember? I'd unconsciously try to start arguments to drive my partners away. Eventually, I'd start sending messages about how depressed and anxious I was. Yeah, it was a lot for people to deal with, but my strategy worked. I had a pretty high success rate for driving people away.

When I met Alicia, the same old game played out. The relationship was going really well, so I fell right back into self-sabotage mode, constantly trying to drive her away. We were running a business together; we had savings, and we were traveling a lot. Basically, we were on top of the world. However, the better our lives got, the more my mental health deteriorated. The deeper into our relationship we went, the realer it became. The realer it became, the more I tried to sabotage it.

When we got engaged, I began falling off that all too familiar cliff. I started drinking again and was eating a lot of junk food. The commitment of engagement and the marriage that would follow were too real for me. It wasn't the commitment itself that triggered me – it was the belief that I wasn't good enough for Alicia. If we went through with the marriage, she'd be stuck with me. With my self-worth so low, I thought she deserved more. I thought she deserved *better*.

So, I sabotaged the relationship in any way I could: sleeping on the couch, recklessly spending money, not going to work, taking off for extended periods with the boys – the list goes on. None of these actions aligned with my values and the way I wanted to live my life, but I couldn't break the pattern. Self-sabotage had been my go-to play for so long that I struggled to imagine another way forward.

Looking back, I can analyse each situation and understand exactly what I was doing. The self-sabotage is glaringly evident. But I didn't have that awareness at the time, which was a big part of the problem. Unconscious thoughts and beliefs were driving a lot of my actions. I couldn't stop the self-destructive behaviour because I lacked awareness around what I was doing. Why was I sabotaging every opportunity that came my way? Why did my mental health go to shit every time I started to do well? Why did I drive people away when relationships got too real? At the time, I didn't have the understanding to answer those questions, so I continued to play the self-sabotage game.

Regarding my self-sabotaging behaviour, I didn't intend to do a lot of what I did, and my actions during those times don't sit well with me. I felt a lot of shame and guilt around those instances, which made the whole situation worse. Now, however, when I start down that familiar path of self-sabotage, thanks to the help and advice I've received over the years, I'm aware of what's happening, which means I can head off destructive behaviour before it becomes a major problem… most of the time. I know I need to be vigilant. If I let my guard down for a moment, I could find myself drinking to excess, taking drugs, staring at screens for hours on end, refusing to sleep – all behaviours I've added to my self-sabotage toolkit over the years.

For the people around us, especially those who care about us, knowing how to deal with this type of behaviour can be difficult. Even now, Alicia sometimes tries to build me up when I'm feeling down. What she, and others, struggle to understand is that all the kind words and compliments in the world don't matter, regardless of how true they are, because the internal voice of self-doubt is much, much louder. When people heap too much praise on me, it can actually be detrimental to my mental health. To anyone who hasn't experienced that mindset, it may not make a lot of sense, but it's how my brain works. Success doesn't align with my internal beliefs so when someone implies I'm doing well, I unconsciously try to correct course towards failure because that's what I think I deserve. Not exactly the ideal way to navigate life, is it? Nope, not even close.

Thankfully, Alicia saw past my shitty behaviour, and we made it to the altar. "In sickness and in health…" We all know the classic wedding vow. I think Alicia would agree that the line is as real as it gets when you're married to someone who has mental health challenges. Whenever I'm having a rough time, she's right there, riding the waves with me. Multiple times, I pushed her to the brink, but somehow she stuck it out.

The key for us has been open communication. I've told her, "If this isn't working for you, you need to walk away." Part of me wants her to walk away – but that's the self-saboteur talking. *I don't deserve this* is a common thought that crosses my mind. But I also think, *She doesn't deserve this.* That's the other dark side of this belief system: you don't think they deserve it either. They don't deserve the trouble you're putting them through. They deserve better. The thing is, Alicia is a grown adult, and she's more than capable of making her own decisions. It's something I've had to come to terms with. If she chooses to be with me, who am I to tell her she's wrong?

During our relationship, we've had some amazing times, but we've also had some really dark moments. Being able to talk about anything and everything with Alicia has been so important. I reached a point where I had to choose to either keep going down the same route of self-sabotage or reach out, get help, and try to understand where these destructive belief systems came from. Why did I believe I wasn't worthy of success and happiness? Once I understood these core beliefs better, I then had to work through them.

Day to day, we carry so many negative beliefs around with us, beliefs we picked up in childhood and never analysed or addressed. Over time, they gather and pile on top of each other, and sorting through them all becomes even more of a challenge. Honestly, we probably can't change them all, but we can work on the ones that are affecting us the most.

When you're in a relationship, you're working on those beliefs together. I love the quote, "We'll always love each other, but we won't always like each other." Alicia and I won't always agree with each other or support each other's behaviour, but that's okay because our love is unconditional. It's always there, and it has helped us ride out the lows and even navigate some of the highs. As we know, when something is going well, if I drop my guard, I'm going to try to stuff it up. The difference now is that when it happens, we both understand what's going on and why. When I slide into self-sabotage mode, we slow down and avoid making any big decisions until I come out the other side.

Did you know that as little as 5 percent of what we do is based on conscious decisions? The rest is driven by our subconscious, the mysterious and unconscious parts of the brain that we have little control over. It's no wonder it's so easy to fall back into familiar yet destructive patterns. It's no wonder positive change takes a *lot* of conscious effort. You can't expect to overcome those ingrained belief systems and experience a massive transformation in a blink. As Alicia and I have learnt, these things take time, effort, and perseverance.

Occasionally, I do start to fall back into that familiar, dark hole, but we've got much better at pulling me out of it. Mostly, it's due to recognising *when* I'm in that hole. Once we know that's where I am, we can figure out what we need to do to get me out again. We don't always get it right, but we understand that mistakes are a necessary part of the journey. They're where the real learning occurs.

I have a tendency to throw money at courses, projects, and other ventures and never complete them. The self-sabotage almost always kicks in and derails any progress. When I started writing this book, Alicia feared I was starting another big, important project that I wouldn't see through. Honestly, she was almost right. I definitely had the urge to self-sabotage and pull the plug on this book several times throughout the process, especially towards the end when it started to get real, when it started to get *really* real. That's just my default mode of operation. Thankfully, I'm learning to overcome that programming, and, evidently, I did push through to the finish line to release this book into the world. This time, the project was too important, and failure *wasn't* an option.

COMBATTING THE SELF-SABOTEUR MINDSET – WHAT WORKS FOR ME

When I go into self-sabotage mode, I tend to shut down a bit. I know that nothing I say or do will help the situation, so I've learnt to create some space to avoid unnecessary arguments with the people around me. Later, when I'm ready, I can restart the conversation with a clearer head and a clean slate.

For me, the biggest game changer has been healthy, honest communication – and communication is a two-way street. If I'm feeling off and need some space, I can explain this to Alicia, and she understands and knows what to do. And if she notices me starting to fall into that hole before I've realised it myself, she lets me know. Sometimes, I'm unaware of what's happening until I'm deep in self-sabotage mode. But other times, I do catch it early.

For instance, I might realise I've been spending too much time watching TV, which doesn't align with my family values. So, I tell Alicia, and we make a plan to move forward. That way, I have some accountability. When I do set boundaries, she's really good at helping me stay within them. She knows I struggle with self-control, so she takes the journey with me. For example, if I decide to get in shape and drop a few kilos, we won't have any junk food in the house. Sure, she might have some stashed away in her car, but she's not going to bust it out and eat it in front of me. Essentially, we're in this together.

While everyone is different and I can't say for sure what will help you or a loved one overcome the self-saboteur mindset, I do know that open communication and setting clear boundaries have worked wonders for me.

LIVING WITH DEPRESSION

It's not easy living with someone who has depression or seeing someone close to you suffer. I know because I've seen it firsthand.

It's also not easy living with depression. Some people say it's a choice – it's not! I hate being sad; I hate being miserable, and I hate the fact that sometimes I wake up and don't want to live. However, I rarely have suicidal thoughts anymore, thankfully, which shows how far I've come.

Before I explain how depression isn't a choice, I can understand the view that many choices can contribute to it, but, deep down, there's a lot more to it. The mind is complex, and managing depression generally involves more than just going to the gym, meditating, or eating healthily. Unless you understand this, at some stage, you'll crash and burn, even if it's when you're in your sixties. Or you may live a life pretending you're fine when you're not on the inside.

While I'm not a researcher or anything like that, I understand that the brain relies on habits and routines.

From ages 12 to 25 (possibly even from age five or six, when I thought I was possessed by the devil), I was extremely depressed and suicidal. Now I've found a way out of that, but I felt sad and hated myself for around 20 years of my life.

From the ages of 25 to 29, I found a happiness within myself, and it was great. Then, in mid 2018, it all changed. From that point, it was a slippery slope, which included putting things in place that failed. I tried and tried and tried to change without successfully regaining the happiness I'd had and lost.

Each time I didn't succeed, I saw myself as a failure. It's clear that even though I've dramatically improved, it's very easy to fall back into old thinking patterns after a few triggers and challenging situations. It reached a point where I couldn't see how anything could change the way I was feeling.

In October of 2019, I realised it was time to get the care and support I needed and put everything into me. This was the hardest and scariest decision I'd ever had to make because I care so much about others, and I didn't want to let anyone down. But the fact is, I had to do this to get myself in a position where I could help and care for others. This decision and what I needed to do to work on myself went against society's belief that men should just suck it up.

I decided, with the help of professionals and people close to me, that I'd be going away indefinitely to work on my internal issues and get to the root cause. It took a lot of thought and action on behalf of myself and my support network to decide what was best for me.

At the time, I wasn't sure what it was going to look like – it could have been a mental health clinic or a trip to a friend's place in another state. It could have been expensive or cheap, but those things weren't what mattered. The only thing that mattered was that it was the best thing for me and for sorting through my issues. I couldn't run or hide from them. I had to hit them head-on.

Depression is more complex than a solution that comes in the form of a pill or a gym session, but those things can help. The truth is, at that point in my life, there was only one thing that got me out of bed, and that was the charity cricket match for mental health I was organising. It meant so much to me, and I hated that it was the only thing that motivated me. It was also why I struggled some days when nothing was happening with it, or when I was waiting on things to be organised or sent to me, which was out of my control.

I wanted to *want* to get out of bed for other things, but even showers were completely forced. At the time, I knew my family and friends were hurting, and I tried to use that as motivation. I was hurting too because I hated how I was. Trust me, it wasn't easy.

It's okay to get support and ask for help. Do it – before it's too late. It's important to share how you're feeling. No matter how dark it gets, I stay true to me and share, to help myself and others. Keep working on yourself day after day, week after week, year after year.

Instead of putting myself through more pain and unnecessary suffering when I was at my lowest in 2019, I chose to do something about it.

My inpatient stay could have cost me and my family over $40k, but, in the end, we had to make choices. It was hard, but I assure you, there's always a way.

Part of our way of dealing with it was communicating and putting everything on the table. We had to handle the reality of the situation, and the first part of that was having the hard conversations.

INVESTING IN YOURSELF IS ALWAYS WORTH IT

After reaching breaking point in 2019, I walked into a mental health clinic. I was scared when I walked through the doors but when Alicia drove off, it really hit home. *Am I really doing this?* But, like I said, I was at breaking point, and I needed to make a change, or I wasn't going to survive, not with things the way they were. Ultimately, investing in myself changed my life.

A combination of things led to my downward spiral. Mainly, I wasn't able to manage my thoughts and emotions. There were also still a lot of things that I needed to heal that weren't healed yet.

I also knew that, like anyone who genuinely wants to work on their mental health, I really needed to invest time and finances to be accountable. The financial side of my treatment included four weeks off work, which probably cost $4,000, plus the treatment itself, which cost $1,000. There were extra expenses as well. I spent between $1,500 and $2,000 on outside therapy with Ryan from the Centre for Healing. When I finished my treatment at the mental health clinic, I spent a few more thousand dollars on therapy over that year. I had to do that for myself. It wasn't a choice – it was a necessity.

To afford it all, I had to sell some of my belongings and take out loans, and Alicia and I put our business on the line. I'm thankful that our hard work allowed me some financial flexibility but even if we didn't have that freedom, I was prepared to find a way because the cost if I didn't would've been much worse.

In the 12 months prior, I hadn't been working properly because I was sleeping all the time. I'd struggle through coaching footy and then go home to sleep on the couch. I was sleeping 20 hours a day, wanting to die. I wasn't a good friend because I didn't think I deserved anyone. I was eating bucket loads of Uber Eats, and I was drinking. With the way I was living, I was costing myself so much more financially. I was costing us our savings.

So, if I didn't spend $20k and three or four months really working on this stuff, I probably would've spent $150k in the next year on crap anyway. Clearly, I had to do something because shiny objects, fast food, alcohol, and drugs weren't going to help my happiness and health. I had no other choice but to act because not only was I bringing myself down, but I was bringing everyone else around me down as well.

I had many fears about walking into that hospital. I felt like there was judgement and fear around being 'crazy'. People knew that, over the past five years, I'd been running a really successful personal training business and I'd met Alicia. Everyone would've assumed I was fine – but I wasn't. For this reason, putting my hand out for help was especially hard. I was ruining the illusion that everything was fine.

Over the next month, I went to the mental health clinic and saw an external specialist. Both cost money, but that money was an investment – an investment with a pay-off that was much more than financial. So, what did I gain?

In return, I saved my relationship and married the love of my life.

In return, it gave me the strength to work through finding out I was infertile, going through the IVF process, and having our first child together.

In return, it gave me skills to manage my emotions much more effectively so I didn't harm friendships.

In return, it gave me lots more composure while playing sport.

In return, it allowed me to work through the many challenges that have arisen in recent years.

In return, I finally understood that true happiness is internal and to stop chasing external sources looking for it. I've seen so many people, including myself, fall prey to this, which causes problems, as external sources can change daily. A lot of the time, we can't control that, but we can control ourselves.

If you need help, please reach out and take the hard path to find the internal happiness you deserve. The financial investment and hard work are more than worth it. Some of this help is even accessible at no cost or at a low cost for those who are ready to step into that space.

THE WORK NEVER STOPS

I've experienced so much darkness, but I've also done so much work on my mental health that often people question how I could've done all of this work but still not be mentally well. This meant that when I realised I needed help again in November of 2019, it was really difficult to walk into a hospital and admit that I wasn't well.

I had a funny moment when someone said to me, "You'll walk out, and nothing in the world will have changed except your perception of it." It was so true; nothing had changed. It was actually quite frustrating because I thought things *would* change. However, it was all about how I perceived the world. Everyone was still carrying on with their lives, and it kind of makes you realise how insignificant you are in a way. You can have whatever going on mentally, but, in reality, life does keep going on. It has to.

This feeling is relieving, but it's also distressing. I came out of hospital different, and part of this was knowing that I can't ever stop working on myself.

CHAPTER 7

WHAT I HAVE LEARNT

HOPE, RECOVERY, AND RESILIENCE

As you now know, at the age of 21, I ended up in hospital after attempting to take my own life. As a male, I grew up believing that speaking about my struggles would earn the judgement of others, and the impact this had on my mental health was immense.

To put everything in perspective, I had a loving, supportive family, a roof over my head, great friends, and fulfilling hobbies, mainly sports. I was involved in any sport the school put on, and I hung out with friends often. From the outside, it looked like nothing was wrong at all.

As the years went by, my self-confidence and self-esteem deteriorated. I would blow up about the small things, and I couldn't deal with emotionally hurting someone else. In response, I would run, scream, and self-harm.

My family and friends thought I was overreacting, and I agree. I was seeking attention because I wanted help and had no idea how to ask for it. I certainly had no idea how to help myself. My suicidal thoughts and nightmares worsened, and I was lost in a completely negative world inside my own head.

As you know, after growing up wanting to be an actor, I pulled out of my final drama assessment in year 12 and locked myself in a cupboard for eight hours because I was scared of being judged on stage – not an ideal feeling for someone wanting to be an actor.

After school, things just got worse. It was, in part, because of a lack of structure in my life. Heavy drinking became a weekly occurrence to mask the pain I was experiencing, but it would only work for a couple of hours. By 1 am on a Sunday morning, the suicidal thoughts would be more real and scary than ever.

Sometimes, when I hit that specific red light on my way to work at Hungry Jacks, I'd spend nine hours parked in a side street, crying without knowing why before driving home and pretending nothing had happened.

Evidently, my two major triggers are relationships with women and money, and issues in both these spheres led to my suicide attempt at age 21. When I was diagnosed with depression in the hospital, it was a relief to learn I wasn't 'crazy'.

What happened next was so surprising to me because I had felt so alone for so long. Suddenly, I had support from so many people. While I've slowly lost some friends from childhood, the response was primarily one of support, and the people who stayed in my life are so important to me.

Support came in many ways. It was rarely someone wanting to directly speak about my feelings. Instead, it was the small things. Friends would offer to take me to a footy game or kick the footy in the local park. I'd get texts that simply checked in on what had been happening in my life. For me, it was enough to know that people were trying.

I think that because of my depression and how I handled it, I wasn't easy to deal with – I was so negative. However, the moment I was diagnosed, I realised something: I was at rock bottom, and anything and everything going forward would be an improvement.

After my hospital visit and diagnosis, I was off to see a psychologist. I went once and felt great – I was cured! But, oh boy, was I wrong. Truth be told, I was so scared to open up about everything and was still terrified of judgement.

Time went by, and so did psychologist number two and three. I was getting advice and guidance, but I wasn't acting on it. Simply, I wasn't helping myself.

Friends started to drift away. Because they were trying to help me, watching me not help myself and ignoring the help of others frustrated them. The psychologists, my family, and my friends were basically banging their heads against a brick wall.

A couple of years went by, and I experienced more failed relationships. A few friends drifted out of my life, and I realised it would only get worse if I didn't finally try to help myself.

At the time of writing, it has been eleven years since I attempted to take my own life, and they've been challenging years, but they've given me the life I live today. Once I accepted that I was in my position because of my own choices and I needed help, things finally started to change. I'd be lying if I said it happened overnight, as this has been a gradual journey.

It was my fifth psychologist who finally got through to me. Too many people give up on speaking to a professional after one or two failed attempts, but it's important to think about a few things while finding someone to help you. Firstly, do you get along with everyone in the world? No! So, don't expect that the first, second, or sometimes even the tenth professional is for you. Your values need to match to an extent, but you must be honest with them and give it a chance (and one session isn't a chance).

Currently, I see a psychologist, use mental health techniques that work for me, and create healthy habits and routines that help me with my happiness and health.

Have I relapsed? Many times. My mental health is like a rollercoaster ride, with great highs and big lows. Each low is a lesson, and, instead of beating myself up, I accept it and learn. Each high is something to take hold of and keep in the memory bank for when a low comes and I need a reminder that happiness exists.

Decades of depression and anxiety are hard to summarise, but I'm determined to share my story to show that there's hope for anyone and everyone. My story is only one of hundreds I know of success despite mental illness. Survivors and people who succeed through these struggles are strong and work hard, and every single one of you can succeed as well – I promise you.

MINE IS A STORY OF HOPE

I still have suicidal thoughts sometimes but with the work I've done on myself, I have the ability to understand them and manage them so they don't have the power to scare me anymore.

To show you there's hope, I'd like to share what I've achieved over several years, despite my mental health issues:

- I completed a landscaping apprenticeship and worked as a subcontractor for three years.

- I completed two beginner acting courses and did work as an extra for *Neighbours*, Sportsbet, and Pepsi.
- I started a blog to share my story and things that have helped me and others.
- I've done suicide prevention videos for Beyond Blue.
- I was a volunteer speaker for Beyond Blue and have done over one hundred talks to groups, with audiences from high school students to sporting clubs to RSL members. Since trying to take my own life, I've been open with my story, which has encouraged so many people to come to me and share their stories – stories that even their parents or partners might not have known yet. I want that stigma to be reduced.
- I have my own personal training business, which involves an online coaching program. This was a dream I followed after getting fit myself and gaining lots of strength and fitness. This experience gave me so much confidence and helped me mentally, so I quit my job and started the business to help others in the same situation.
- I've started a podcast to both share my own story, help others share their stories, and help and inspire others.
- I'm now a husband and a dad, which I'll touch more on later.

I survived, and I know it was to break down the stigma and show hope to others. I'm not a hero; I'm just normal, but I know I can help others. It's not easy, but I know it's my purpose in life.

What I've learnt is that, firstly, you have to want to help yourself, then take it one step at a time. The feeling of being overwhelmed makes things worse, and I think we can all relate to that. So, focus on one task and get that done before moving on to the next one. Don't look for 'the answer'. So many of us have been there at some stage, where the pain of where we are is too much, so we try to take the easy path. But that easy path to a 'quick fix' creates a hard life. Instead, when we step outside of our comfort zone, challenge ourselves with empathy, and take the hard path, we create much easier lives for ourselves.

These days, I rely on no one but myself, and I have a lot of management skills and strategies to get me back on track when I'm in a low. I don't believe in one method being the answer – it's important to have many tools to help you.

In addition to medication and a psychologist, I've realised that I need many different avenues to get me through tough times. My strategies include:

- My family
- Reading
- Writing
- Work
- Study
- My pets
- Walking
- Running
- Training
- Friends
- Hikes
- TV
- Comedy
- Helping others
- Eating well

There are many tools we can use to help our mental health, and I'll discuss making a list like this for yourself in a later chapter.

Remember, you are worth it. You are enough. You can get through this. You are strong enough.

REDISCOVERING MY PURPOSE

Part of my healing was also finding a sense of purpose again. While I was in the mental health clinic, even though I was unwell, I could still see how unwell other people were. Probably my greatest gift (but also my greatest detriment) is seeing other people in pain and wanting to help. One day, a nurse sat with me for around two hours. She just listened to me and cared, and I realised that I do that for other people too. This impacted me intensely, and I realised that's what I wanted to continue doing with my life. I needed to be well to do this, so it gave me purpose and drive again.

There were people in the hospital who I connected with, who were able to open up to me, and we formed supportive friendships. I'm still in touch with a few of them, and I see them doing really well, but some aren't doing well. They're in that cycle of going in and out of mental health clinics and good and bad periods. I've been in that cycle, and it breaks my heart to see other people experiencing it and struggling.

That's what really drove me. There are so many amazing people out there, and being able to talk to them and help them is what I want. I love talking about this raw stuff with people because I know it helps them – that's why I started the podcast. Regardless of how long they talk, it gets all this stuff off their chests, and they walk away feeling lighter. After walking out of the clinic, I had purpose, passion, drive, and routine again.

My experience also gave me so much respect for the nurses, doctors, and health professionals. Some people will criticise and get angry at them because of their demeanour and how they work. However, they've been working in this field for so long; they've seen so much, and they're probably burnt out while trying to do their best. We all have to understand that these people are just humans too. We're all humans with emotions and stuff that goes on.

I learnt tools and strategies from my stay in the mental health clinic, and the most significant tool was routine. Essentially, once I came to terms with what I was working on mental health wise, the first thing I realised was that routine was imperative.

When my mental health is struggling, routine comes down to the basics, like showering and brushing my teeth. In the clinic, I made a rule for myself that I had to get up for breakfast before 7 am every morning. After that, it was up to me to figure out how the day was going to go. There were group sessions throughout the day, as well as a walk, gym sessions, and therapy sessions. I made a point of just making sure I got up and ate breakfast. Usually, the rest of my day would follow.

The other main part of my routine was that I gave my phone to the nurses to put away from 8 pm until 4 pm, so, every day, for a 20-hour period, I didn't have my phone. That changed as I progressed through the treatment because I started talking to more friends and family on the outside, but I knew how important it was for me. Because I didn't have my phone, I had to do something else to keep engaged, so it motivated me.

Getting to breakfast by 7 am and not having my phone were the two things that made the rest of it work. Going through this has really taught me that you just need one or two things to kick off your routine, and the rest of the day will follow.

Whenever things start to slip away, I always go back to those simple things I learnt in there. I really try to enforce the routine, even though it's much harder in the real world. We've got so many distractions with partners, kids, friends, family, work, and hobbies, but we need to stick to the basics to be our best for ourselves and the people around us. Even though I need a bit of flexibility, I also need some form of routine; otherwise, I get overwhelmed. I can live a really busy life, but I need to have a routine.

EFFECTIVE STRATEGIES ARE INVALUABLE

In addition to finding my purpose again and learning the importance of routine, my stay in the mental health clinic taught me many valuable lessons and strategies.

Journalling was something I practised a lot throughout treatment. It really allowed me to get all the irrational thoughts out of my head, giving me the capacity to think without fogginess, which created a safer space for me. There were other benefits too, which is why I created a wellbeing and accountability journal for others.

In group therapy sessions, I learnt three valuable lessons from the therapist. The first thing I learnt is that everyone has subconscious stuff that dictates much of their lives. The therapist told us about a client he'd had in the past who was a hoarder and also very overweight. The therapist went to the client's house for an appointment, and, because of his hoarding, the house was set up so only one person could walk in every hallway, door, around the bed, everywhere. The client could only just fit around the house. The therapist started to gently dive into his client's hoarding and the reasoning behind it. He asked the client about whether he had been hurt before and got to the bottom of the trauma. This client was gay and had been so judged and mistreated because of it, so he decided it was just easier to be alone. Everything in his life was dictated by only being able to have one person there. So, the hoarding came from this deep, subconscious belief that being gay wasn't a good thing. Finding someone (like a partner) meant he had to open up his world, but that had gone badly in the past, so he shut down on the outside. From that story, I learnt that people always do things for a reason. Always.

Secondly, we were sitting there in a group session, and the therapist asked, "Where do you think all of the emotions we have come from?" We all started throwing out reasons why we might feel the way we do, such as anger, frustration, sadness, annoyed, lost, confused, other people, but we didn't get to the root of it. The therapist listened to all of our answers and said, "Everything you've put out there stems from one thing. You are hurt. That's all it is. Somewhere along the line of your life, you've been hurt, and that has stuck with you and become a trigger. People don't show anger because they're angry, it's because they're hurt. If you get to the root of what's going on, we're all just hurt." The more I try to debunk that, the more I find it's real.

The third lesson I learnt is that we, as humans, like to make things as easy as possible without knowing it. The therapist got us all to stand up behind our chairs, and he ran the start of the session while we stood like that. Five minutes later, he told us to take a look around the room and asked us what had changed. We had no idea. He explained, "You're all leaning on the chairs." He'd told us to stand, not lean, but we're creatures who want things to be as easy as possible, so we'd subconsciously leant on the chairs without realising. This told me a lot about us as humans, particularly when our mental health isn't doing well. When we're struggling, we stick to our comfort zone, and it can be so easy to get caught up in this and not leave the couch, or not eat, or binge eat to get through. We're conditioned to save as much energy as possible, but it takes energy to work on ourselves.

WE CAN HELP OURSELVES

Stress, anxiety, and frustration can all creep in at times, and that's normal – they're human emotions. I had to learn to manage these feelings, and I've worked on them in therapy, with someone who tells me what I need to hear, not what I want to hear.

I learnt meditation and discovered that, previously, I hadn't been truly meditating – I'd been relaxing, contemplating, or ruminating. I now meditate a couple of times a week, which helps me immensely. I also journal when my head feels foggy and I feel like I can't think. Additionally, I started weight training again and set some mini goals to help my overall mind and body health. I also got a traineeship and followed my passion and purpose at MyndFit, which gave me a sense of belonging.

The number one thing I've learnt is not to put my happiness or sadness in the hands of other people, things, or institutions, like the government or my job or my sport. It has to start internally. First and foremost, it must come from within. I've learnt not to outsource my happiness and not to rely on others for it.

Life will happen – every day, every week, every year – and every time it does, we have the choice. We can either adapt and change with it, or get stuck, complain, and ultimately live a life of unhappiness.

I'm not a hero for doing any of the work I do. All I did was ask for help, and I was completely honest and took an extremely hard and uncomfortable path. Anyone can do this – I'm not special at all.

> *"When one door closes, another opens."*
> – Alexander Graham Bell

One of the big things I do for myself is make a list of some of the things I can do daily and weekly to keep myself at peace, as I understand that the only person who can ruin my life is me.

SPORT IS STILL AN OUTLET

Recently, I went to watch a mate receive his lifetime membership at Mooroolbark Football Club, and something he said stuck with me. I don't remember his exact words, but it was along the lines of, "Our kids will be involved in sporting clubs too." He was talking about the people you meet and the support you get from sporting clubs and how important that is for us.

Over the years, I've worked my backside off, every night and every morning. Because of that, I had to stop playing footy, and my cricket time was limited too. For three and a half years, I struggled with my depression and anxiety, but not to the extent I did when I was younger in my worst times. Sometimes, I felt crazy because I felt like something was missing, and I didn't know what it was. I loved my business, and I loved the work I was doing, which motivated me to work as hard as I could.

When I started my personal training business in 2016, I'd been working 80 hours a week, and I restricted a lot of my life. During this period, I kept doing it because I thought it was the way it had to be. A client would ask to change a session or session time, and I'd say yes because I'd allow clients to change anything, just to please them. I'd sit with a client for ages and make sure they were okay. I'd go out of my way for anyone in the business because I felt like I had to, and, quite often, it didn't change anything, which broke my heart. None of this was anyone's fault but mine – it's the people pleaser in me.

Since then, I've cut it down because I started to understand that if I do the huge work weeks, my family, friends, and I get the rest of me and not the best of me. Finding a balance is key and even more so now as a parent. Over several months, I found my way back to the life I love, the one that aids my mental health. One of the things that helps me the most is sporting clubs.

Sporting clubs are like big families, and the support is immense. The impact of not being involved in them for a few years broke me down so much more than I realised. This was a huge learning curve for me.

There are two main reasons why I play sport. The first is premierships — because winning is fun. But as amazing as winning a premiership is, there's a more important reason why I play sport: friendship, community, and support. At a sporting club, there's always someone you can turn to for help. People will always have your back, even if they don't always agree with what you're doing. I've learnt more about life in sporting clubs than anywhere else.

Even with premierships, the best thing about them is winning them with the people you care about and those who care about you — that's what makes it feel so special. You know how hard each person worked for it and how much they've overcome to be there in the end, holding the premiership cup.

It's simple: if it wasn't for the sporting clubs I've played for and been a part of, I wouldn't be here.

Without a doubt, my kids will be born into sporting clubs. Obviously, it won't be forced onto them, but I have no doubt they'll fall in love with sporting clubs straight away because they'll see the fun, love, and care involved, and those things are infectious.

My passions for sport and mental health can align, and I want mental health to become a number one priority in all sporting clubs. It will attract more and more people to the clubs and help eliminate the stigma around mental health in sporting communities.

For you or your loved one, it might not be a sporting club but something else that provides love, community, and connection for the individual in need. Love, community, and connection are part of the recipe for great wellbeing.

POWER, STRENGTH & VULNERABILITY

After my suicide attempt, I was very open about my mental health diagnosis and the fact that I'd battled a lot of these issues for around ten years. From there, I had many people who I looked up to come to me and share their stories. These were some of the best footballers in the local leagues, who had great jobs and amazing families.

I'd always ask, "Does anyone know about your depression and suicidal tendencies?" Not one person over the first three months of speaking to people responded with a yes. Every time, they were battling their mental health issues completely alone, and those moments taught me that my ability to speak up gave others a voice.

These men quite often said that speaking to me or reading what I'd shared gave them confidence to speak to their families and get further help with their issues. It was then that I made the decision to continue to share openly, to help as many people as possible who were struggling with their own mental health.

Fast forward a few years – after many speaking events with Beyond Blue, I decided to create a Facebook blog, which gained great traction. Then, after over 120 speaking events, years of running the blog, and speaking individually to thousands of people about their struggles, I got extremely burnt out from the continual giving.

I loved helping, and I loved having a voice that allowed people to get the help they needed or for them to ultimately feel like they weren't alone. I just needed to make some changes to how I went about this – and that's when Power, Strength & Vulnerability was created to allow more structure and focus but to ultimately create something that wasn't just about me.

I then started a podcast to share other people's stories and help listeners understand that these uncomfortable conversations *can* happen with friends and family members, and it can help. While these conversations about our struggles are uncomfortable, they're completely necessary to allow our minds clarity day to day. By speaking up and speaking out, along with the clarity, it creates a united movement forward.

When speaking up and speaking out, you'll also find others who have battled or are battling very similar things to you, and that can be quite comforting in the healing process.

Power, Strength & Vulnerability is a breakdown of what is needed for an individual to change their life. The **power** to make the necessary changes to create the desired life, the **strength** to continually overcome life's challenges, and the **vulnerability** to open ourselves up creates this amazing space. Harnessing strength and power helps us create and live the ultimate lives.

The podcast itself is about harnessing everything PSV is built on, with guests sharing their stories and opening themselves up with great vulnerability, strength, and power. This gives listeners some great insight into how others get through their struggles.

MENTAL HEALTH IMPACTS RELATIONSHIPS

As men, it's so hard to talk about our feelings in a society that tells us not to. We all want to surround ourselves with people who understand and can help us learn and deal with things, but open and honest communication isn't easy.

It's hard to see our loved ones who are struggling or to be struggling while our loved ones watch us. There's a lot of guilt and stress on both sides, particularly around serious consequences of mental health issues.

In my own experience, if someone wants to kill themselves, there's nothing anyone can do to stop them. Loved ones of someone who does kill themselves often go through thoughts like, *What could I have done? What should I have done? I should have been there. Maybe it's my fault because I didn't do enough to help them or stop them.* They punish themselves with these thoughts. However, we all need to recognise that when someone is in that headspace, there's nothing we can really do. Even when you try your hardest, there's nothing you can do. Maybe you could have got through in all the other moments. But in that moment, no. We all need to understand that someone else's actions are not our fault – we have no control. We can't do anything about it, so we can't feel guilty, and we can't take that on. It's *not* ours to take on.

It's important to think about what they're struggling with and what they're going through, as well as what you're going through and how you're feeling. It's not just thinking about yourself but also trying to understand the other person.

As the person who's struggling with their mental health or the loved one watching on and trying to support them, it's nice for both people to have someone they can have open dialogue with. Surround yourself with people who are emotionally intelligent. Even listening to podcasts, watching YouTube videos, or reading books that are relevant to mental health can do so much for expanding knowledge and creating a sense of community.

I talked most about my suicidal thoughts with girls when I was growing up. I'd make it really clear that none of my struggles were their fault, but I dumped all of my feelings on them, particularly when I got drunk. I'd get into relationship-type situations, and my behaviour and mental health would be extreme. I'd be really suicidal, often running away from friends' houses and disappearing. I'd engage in incredibly risky behaviour, like drink driving, to get what I wanted.

The girls who I was in these situations with all left me, and I'm so glad they did. Every time, it broke me and made me worse in the short-term, but, long-term, leaving me was the best thing they could have done.

I remember being 16 or 17, crying in the bathtub because a girl broke up with me. Then when I was older, I turned to drinking, drugs, and really reckless behaviour. However, these women putting boundaries in place for themselves was the best thing for everyone in the long-term because it forced me to change. Here I was, a young man. My dream was to be a dad, and everyone I dated was leaving me. I realised that if I didn't change my behaviour and work on myself, I wouldn't get my dream. If these women hadn't left me and cut me out, and instead let me continue behaving how I was, it would have enabled my behaviour. There's no way I would be here today, because it would have gotten worse.

I was definitely putting myself in positions where I was extremely vulnerable to being hurt. There were a few moments when someone did what they needed to do, and I didn't feel safe because I was very suicidal. I'm not proud of this, and it wasn't healthy or fair on others.

I was being genuine in wanting to take my own life, but the way it came across was so unhealthy. I didn't understand that at the time. Even with Alicia, the reality when I walked into the mental health clinic was that if I didn't change the way she needed me to, she had to leave me because I wasn't treating her well. There was a level of understanding there, and, unfortunately, it was a form of emotional abuse that had been happening when I was at my worst. I've come to realise that now, and I'm so glad I was able to get help, both for myself and for Alicia. It has put us in a better position now, and those toxic behaviours don't happen anymore.

So often, when someone is going through mental health issues, they can say or do things that harm the people around them, and the statistics around domestic and family violence really undersell the reality of what's happening for so many people. We often excuse people's behaviour because they have mental health complications but if they're not actually getting help and doing anything about it, that is a form of harm to the people around them. As loved ones of someone who's struggling, we can understand it and accept it but if they're not getting help, you still need to get out. As I said, I'm so grateful to those people I was in relationships with who left me, because it was necessary for both of us.

There's such a stigma around leaving a partner because of their mental health, but it may be necessary and can be empowering to make that decision because it's for the best. You may feel guilty about leaving or bad about putting a boundary in place, but we need to do those things for our own mental health and safety.

UNHEALTHY COPING MECHANISMS

Now when I reflect on how I've dealt with my mental health throughout my life so far, I recognise that I had some really unhealthy coping mechanisms, including drinking and recreational drugs.

In my late teens and early twenties playing footy, we'd celebrate after every game. This meant we'd go to the bottle shop and buy a slab of beer between two people, minimum. It was just habitual. So, while I knew what would happen – I'd get drunk and share about my suicidal thoughts in really unhealthy ways — I felt like I didn't have the ability or option to say, "No, I'm not drinking today" in that period of my life. What came with that was so much worse, and now, in hindsight, I think my friends would have much preferred me to say no to drinking than to end up suicidal at the end of the night.

The longer that dragged on, the more I became aware that drinking wasn't the best thing for me, but I still had the occasional really great night drinking with friends when I wasn't suicidal. Drinking shouldn't be glorified, but you can have fun with it if you're responsible, safe, and healthy about it. Although the nights when I was suicidal were frequent back then, there were still occasional good times when I met really great people.

Over the years, I grew to understand that I couldn't keep doing what I was doing. However, this was more about other people than consideration for myself. I thought that drinking was a problem because it was putting the people around me in bad situations, but I didn't think about what it was doing to me for a number of years. Even when I started being more conscious and responsible with drinking, for me, it still wasn't about my mental health — it was always about taking a break because I had a big game or marathon coming up.

I was 27 when I started really thinking about the relationship between drinking and my mental health, so it was a good ten years of drinking before I went, *Hang on a minute — what's actually happening here?* Even if I was drinking more responsibly and taking breaks, if

I wasn't in a good headspace when I did drink, it made me feel a lot worse.

Now, I won't drink at all if I'm not in a good headspace – it's just a no-go. If I know there's an event coming up, like a big celebration or a weekend away with team mates, I'll be really conscious for the three or four weeks leading up to make sure I look after my mental health. I know I need to be in the best headspace possible to be healthy and happy and have those experiences safely and responsibly.

Personally, I'm not a believer in giving up things. I believe you can enjoy things in moderation and control them in healthy ways. Obviously, there are people who struggle with addiction and can't control that, and that's okay. But, in my case, I'm able to control things like drinking and gambling. With gambling, I spend $40–50 a week when the footy is on but when it's not, I don't even open the app.

All of these things that we can do are just part of life. They're not bad things; it's our relationships with them that can be healthy or unhealthy. For me, what helps me do things in a healthy way is making sure I'm in a good headspace, and I'll be honest – I don't always get that right. I've done a lot of work on myself and learnt how to deal with mental health in a productive way, but sometimes it can be difficult to act in accordance with that, which is okay. I'm not perfect.

For example, there was an incident in 2020 during the lockdowns that really emphasises how much I don't like hurting other people. A few friends and I got together for drinks, and, a few hours into the night, I drunkenly vomited onto my mate's back. Obviously, he was quite upset about it, and my instinct was to get out of there. I got home at 3 or 4 am, and Alicia was up waiting for me. I just went to bed because I needed space and sleep and to sober up before I could deal with it in a healthy way.

It wasn't just about me stuffing up for myself. What I was struggling with was what I'd done to potentially hurt my friendship, and that's why I felt my behaviour was inexcusable. I thought that I let my friends down, so I automatically thought they hated me. This old mindset came right back because it's still the default system within me, instinctively going to those thoughts.

I get that feeling sometimes from text messages as well, where I'll receive a text and instinctively get this sinking gut feeling that the person on the other end doesn't actually like me, which isn't true. Those thoughts aren't reality.

FEAR COMES IN MANY FORMS

I want to tell you a little story about fear. Growing up, I was the kid who was too scared to ask questions in class, for fear of being wrong. I was the teenager who was too scared to voice my opinion, for fear of being laughed at. I was scared to go for the job promotion, for fear of getting rejected. I was scared to tell stories or jokes to friends, for fear of being ignored. I was scared to commit to a relationship or ask a girl out, for fear of a 'no'. I was scared to ask for help, for fear of being called hopeless. I was scared, and it held me back.

The only time I felt confident to do most of these things was when I was drinking but as soon as I woke up the next day, I felt embarrassed, like I was an idiot.

My worry went so far that I used to say yes to eating things I didn't want to eat or getting drunk because it was 'normal' and saying no felt like letting others down. I worried that getting the body of my dreams would lead to people thinking I was arrogant or up myself. These fears are fears I'm still working through, and fear has affected where I am today. I still get scared that people will see me as an arrogant wanker if I have a sixpack, or they'll think I'm rude if I don't accept the dinner or the beer. I'm learning it's okay to say no. People will understand. These are my own fears, and they're no one's responsibility but mine.

For years, I never achieved what I wanted because I feared what *might* happen. For years, I sat in my comfort zone, and who did it leave unhappy? Me. I couldn't be myself, and it was all because of my own beliefs.

The fact is, we'll all have situations in life that make us feel uncomfortable or nervous, and that's okay. When we push aside the fear and take action, we find out what we're really capable of.

If you want to go out with a girl, ask her on a date! If she says no, at least you can move on. If she says yes, imagine the happiness you'll feel. If you want to get fit, find a coach and start! Don't worry about your mates taking the piss out of you. If you want that promotion, be yourself and own that interview – it will open up a new door, no matter the result.

When you get results and build up your confidence, you'll laugh at yourself for letting fear hold you back. Taking small steps out of your comfort zone breeds success and resilience, and that's power. Learn from everything, be you, and go get your dreams. It's your life, and you live 24/7 with your feelings.

After every photo shoot I've done, I've been worried sick about what my mates would say and how people would judge me on social media. Little did I know that every time I felt that fear, the positive outweighed the negative. People asking me for help or telling me that I've helped inspire them far outweighs any negatives. The support of my family and mates never wavers.

I ALWAYS FELT I WAS DIFFERENT

I have a fear of letting people down, and this has played out throughout my life. As I've worked on my mental health, there has been a lot of ongoing healing and effort around letting go. I don't know where my fear of letting people down started because I always had good friends around me, especially growing up when my mental health struggles started.

I've always felt like I was different from everyone, and I still feel that way. It's not in a negative way; I just have a feeling I'm different. I know I probably am like a lot of people, but other people might not be being honest about who they truly are, so we don't know.

I love watching classic Aussie TV shows like *Neighbours* and *Home and Away*, and I've always loved them. Growing up, when I mentioned interests that weren't socially accepted as 'things boys liked', they were quickly shut down or laughed at. Because of this, I developed a fear that what I talked about was going to be degraded, so I kept quiet as much as I could. I felt that if I opened myself up, I would get criticised, hurt, and degraded again. Now, though, I feel like I can be myself more often, and it's so liberating.

CHAPTER 8

HOW TO HELP YOURSELF

MANAGE YOUR MENTAL HEALTH STRUGGLES

Throughout my life, and particularly in the past few years, I've learnt a bunch of strategies and tools to manage my mental health.

For example, there are a few key strategies I've learnt for taking care of myself. Firstly, use positive reinforcement, such as seeing a therapist even when you're happy, to work on your mental health even when it's good. Secondly, simplify your management skills and routine when you're not well. This means you still have your routine, but you're getting back to the basics and not putting pressure on yourself. Thirdly, do the things you need to do for yourself when you're well so you're consistently creating habits for happiness and fulfilment. Fourthly, do three things for yourself every day. It doesn't matter how big or small they are; it's about making time for yourself.

As I mentioned, I created a journal, and it's centred around the individual looking after themselves holistically. It allows reflection on what can be done to make changes. Doing three things for *you* each day allows you to be a better version of yourself day in, day out, without placing huge expectations on yourself. This has a flow-on effect to everything in your life. It's the way to create positive change in important aspects of your life, including family, friends, work, and hobbies. When you put yourself first, other parts of your life get better.

WHAT MAKES YOU HAPPY?

A major problem with happiness is that, so often, people focus on external factors to create it internally.

For me, it's about going inwards for happiness and making sure I'm empowering myself to be intrinsically happy. This has been a long road, but it's 100 percent worth it.

The benefits of this are endless, but there are two I'd like to focus on:

1. External factors change all the time, and, so often, we don't have control so if we rely on them, it becomes a rollercoaster, and the ride is very tiring. Intrinsic happiness and being empowered means that when external factors change, you have the management skills to keep on top of your emotions.
2. When your happiness comes from within, it radiates with a vibrancy that others pick up, meaning that the external factors become a bonus that puts the cherry on top of your happiness. This leads to better friendships, relationships, jobs, and hobbies.

WHAT IS SUCCESS?

In figuring out how to be happy and manage my mental health, I had to reflect on what success means to me. I suggest this to everyone who wants to work on their life and be content. When

I reflected on passion and success, I realised that despite never having financial abundance, I feel that I've been extremely successful in a way that's much more meaningful to my soul.

Often, we determine success by status, money, or material items, not by relating to the people around us, such as through helping or volunteering. I include myself in that 'we' because it has so often got me down when I haven't been able to afford something. Don't get me wrong, I've done okay financially and had some great opportunities in life, but money isn't my priority. I've spent hours travelling to speaking gigs and never accepted a cent for the travel or the speaking event itself. I didn't want the money – the impact I knew I could have meant so much more to me.

This isn't to brag, but I want to say to you that you don't need money, fame, or material goods to be successful. You need passion. Passion can lead to success, and it can change the world and many people's happiness within our world.

I distinctly remember my first speaking event. At this event, I spoke for 25 minutes, and a famous actor who was the keynote speaker spoke for two 45-minute allotments. Afterwards, a woman from the crowd came up to me and said, "What you said *meant* something. You could hear a pin drop while you were talking. Thank you for sharing it. I've talked to a heap of people here today, and we all wish you had more time to speak, instead of the keynote. He's trying to make himself a big deal, but you will save lives."

A guy from the crowd came up to me as well and explained that he had schizophrenia. He pointed to the table he'd been sitting at and said, "That's my whole family there, and not one of them knows. Your story has given me the inspiration I needed, and I'm going to talk to them about it tomorrow."

Throughout more than 120 speaking events, I've had over 1000 people share their stories with me, ask for a hug, tell me they're going to seek help, or say for the first time they finally felt they could help a family member or friend who was suffering. While I was reflecting on this, I came to the realisation that if I just follow what I love (rather than looking for money), it'll work out – and I truly believe that.

I started reflecting on success because I got so caught up in what people told me I needed in order to be successful that I completely lost myself. I felt trapped; I felt stuck, and I felt like an imposter. I don't blame these mentors who gave me advice because I learnt valuable lessons about what success truly means to me.

My five tips for success are:

1. Have fun! Sometimes, this is hard for me because I can get way too serious, but it's an essential.
2. Don't take things too seriously.
3. Follow your own heart.
4. Don't take what others say personally – they're just doing their best, and it's not a reflection of who *you* are.
5. Follow your passion, and you'll be happy with whatever you get.

My success looks bloody different to what society expects, and I wouldn't change it for the world. Here's to getting back to the roots of what I love and having fun while doing it.

WE COULD ALL USE THERAPY

We should all have a therapist, or at least some type of professional who we speak to about our mental health and what's going on for us — the good and the bad.

It's also really important to go to therapy when you're feeling positive and life is going well. Some of us book into our therapists when we're feeling really down and cancel appointments when we're feeling good, meaning we're missing any positive reinforcement or validation, which we need as human beings. To not go when you're doing well and then to pick it back up when you're not well doesn't make sense to me. It makes so much more sense to also go while we're good for two main reasons. Firstly, consistent work can help prevent downturns. Secondly, it's easier to learn and put strategies in place — and stick to them — when we're well.

My current therapist is someone I can be very open with, and we work really well together. I found him after I spent time in hospital for my mental health. When clients want to cancel appointments, he checks in with them and suggests chatting anyway for positive reinforcement. In most cases, you may as well do the session because it's likely you'll get something good out of it.

During our appointments, sometimes things come up that I don't expect. For example, my therapist will ask how things are going, and

I'll start talking about how I'm feeling really calm and connected – all these great things. He'll listen, reinforce how great that is, and ask what I'm doing to protect and maintain those feelings. Then I'm able to analyse and reflect on what I'm doing to help myself in that moment. This means I'm spending that session reinforcing that work within myself and openly communicating about it, which flows into actually doing it and, again, feeling good about it.

It's always positive reinforcement, which we do need. We're humans who need that positive array of emotions and thoughts. Why do something that's always about the negative? You might just go to therapy monthly, or even quarterly, but it's still important because you're still going. Then if something comes up, you've already got the session there, and that's great. Instead of a super deep, hour-long session about your trauma, it might be more focused on an issue you're facing at the moment. It can be so helpful to talk through what you've learnt in therapy and break all of that down to resolve the issue, and you might not have been able to see that without talking through it. It's like that quote about not being able to see the forest for the trees.

We're emotional human beings, and sometimes we need someone on the outside to help us take a step back and see the bigger picture. Suddenly, within a few minutes of talking, the problem that felt so unfixable or dramatic is overcome with clarity and composure, and you can move forward in a healthy direction. It's hard when you're going well and life's really busy and productive, but you've just got to make the time.

You do your best work when you're feeling good as well. When you're feeling shit, it's unlikely you're going to be productive and do all these great things for your mental health. When you're in a good place, you can do more and be more logical about it, recognising what really works for you and putting those habits in place.

So many people cancel their therapy sessions because they're feeling good, and I wonder why they don't want to tell their therapists about how well they're doing. Likely, they think it's a waste of time and money. So many people think therapy is only about putting out fires instead of learning life skills. But that's an unhealthy relationship; it's really toxic. It's not just about going when you're in a crisis.

That brings us back to the difference between what you do when you're well and what you do when you're not well. Simplifying what you do when you're not well is so important, and trying not to be and do everything is crucial. But when you are well, try not to be everything too. You can't always do everything; you can only do your best.

ROOT CAUSE THERAPY (THE CENTRE FOR HEALING)

I've seen how many different options are out there for people to get assistance, and assistance isn't just bringing someone back from a dark hole. For some, it's about being educated about emotions, seeing a life or business coach, or having a great group of people around them who can play a therapeutic role at times. Other forms of therapy can include sports, art, music, and much more. It doesn't all involve sitting one on one with someone clinical.

I'd also like to mention that seeing a professional as a support person is just as important as anything else. And if you know someone who's struggling and you don't understand them or what they're going through, it might be worth sitting down with an expert and trying to get some insight and assistance for yourself to help the situation.

I've previously mentioned a memory that wasn't accurate, but the trauma sat with me. While I was in hospital in 2019 and after my time in the mental health clinic, I found root cause therapy. It's not a therapy I'd recommend for all, but I had unresolved trauma and trapped emotions I needed to work through. It's important to always find something that helps the individual but also challenges them.

I wanted to change my behaviours so much, and I was willing to give anything a go. My self-sabotage was huge, and, at the Centre for Healing, with my therapist, Ryan, I was able to learn about my conscious and subconscious minds, while learning about how I was lacking when it came to my belief system.

I cried every session, but I was able to let go of so much heaviness that I'd carried around for years. Walking out lighter, with what felt like control of my life and a deep, new-found confidence, allowed me the space to work on a lot of my surface-level issues, as a lot of healing went on beneath the surface. A lot of the pain disappeared, and it wasn't death I wanted anymore. Finding what worked for me took time, but The Centre for Healing played a huge role in helping my deeper mental health issues, rather than my behavioural issues.

STRIKING BALANCE, ALLOWING DOWNTIME

Balance and downtime are also essential. You need to make sure there's a balance of management strategies and activities in your life. To do this, you can be aware and purposeful, with time limits and boundaries around them. For example, going for a run, family time, meditating, journalling, reading, and any other healthy management strategies can become unhealthy.

Balance is about knowing what's good for you and doing those things purposefully. Get into your 'zone', relax, switch off, take time for you to look after you but still with a healthy balance so the rest of your life isn't negatively affected.

As we get older, balance and the way we manage it are different, and that's okay. It's also about finding the balance between feeling really good and ensuring you have downtime you can sit in and appreciate. Because without downtime, you crash. I crash all the time. Even when I'm resting and looking after myself, I can crash.

I've really had to think about what I need to do to take care of myself. There's so much going on in life, with family and work and friends, and then I have to manage myself on top of that. This has changed over the past couple of years, as being married and having kids have changed my priorities and the amount of free time I have. I've struggled with this at points because it can be hard to adjust to big life changes and still prioritise mental health.

In 2021, our son, Ryder, was born, and Alicia's mum got sick and passed away at the same time. Managing having our first kid while grieving was so hard. That's where the journal came in. It helped immensely.

SET YOUR PRIORITIES

Nick from MyndFit taught me a lot, and this task is something I always come back to when I'm starting to feel like I can't manage anymore. I draw a box that's split into four sections to represent the four main things in life: family, friends, hobbies, and work. Then I draw a box in the middle to represent me. Once I've drawn the complete table, I number each box according to its priority in my life. Typically, not many people will put themselves at the top (number one). It's usually family (1), then work (2), then friends (3), then hobbies (4), then you (5). When we're at the bottom, there's so much pressure on us. But when we're on top, we're literally on top of everything. When we prioritise ourselves, we can show up properly and healthily in every area of our lives.

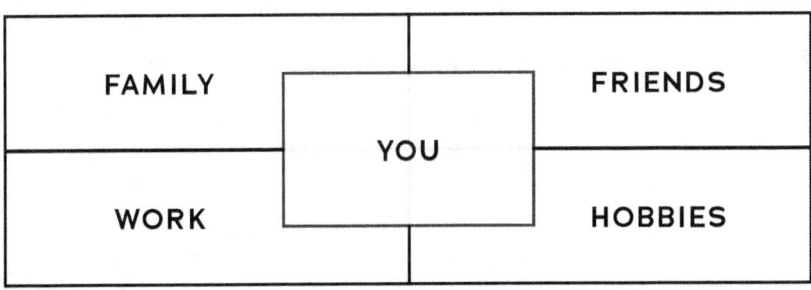

I try as much as I can now to live by that philosophy because, in reality, if I'm good, the people around me will feel the ripple effects of that. If I'm doing poorly, the effects of that also ripple out to the people around me. They feel down and like they're walking on eggshells, like they can't talk to me. If I'm in that state and offering advice to people, how valid is that advice? I can still get in my own way and still have moments that aren't perfect, but balance is essential to doing the best I can.

THREE THINGS, EVERY DAY

Like I said, every single day, whether I'm doing well or not, I do three things for myself.

Meditation is the best. I don't do it enough, and it's hard, but it's important. It's a non-negotiable for me. Journalling is another big one for me. I'll dive deeper into both of these very soon.

Sometimes three things are enough, and sometimes they're not, so it's about being adaptable and flexible. Some days, I wake up to my crying son and my pregnant wife, and what I need becomes irrelevant for an hour or two or three. I can deal with that well if I've looked after myself. If I haven't looked after myself, all of a sudden, I can get frustrated at everyone around me. If you haven't been looking after yourself, you're giving off this bad energy to the people around you, and you're probably not actually helping.

THE DAY I LEARNT THE TRUTH ABOUT MEDITATION

One thing I need to do more, because it's probably the thing that helps me most, is meditation. Although I try to do it often, I don't do it enough.

When I'm not meditating, or even sitting in a state of mindfulness for 10 to 15 minutes a day, I'm usually on a bit of a slippery slope. I'm a lot better at meditating than I was, and I don't need to do it as often as I used to. However, it's still a non-negotiable for me. It's like brushing my teeth.

For example, an athlete doing a triathlon can't only do swimming and riding and not ever run. They have to do all three components because they're all necessities for the race. For my race, my life, meditation is something that needs to happen. There are no buts or maybes about it – it's about finding balance, even though the balance is different now.

I was introduced to meditation by Nick at MyndFit when I started going there in 2020. It was funny because he told me to go into the other room and meditate, so I went in, turned off the light, and laid down on the couch. I heard the door open, and I thought Nick was testing me to see if I failed, but he just asked me what my understanding of meditation was. I said, "Lying down and not thinking."

Nick explained something to me that day, and I thought I best get him to speak more about meditation. Here's what he had to say.

Nick from MyndFit Discusses Meditation

When Shane asked me to write about meditation, I thought, *I can only offer what I know*. I'm not a realised being, holy man, or enlightened one. I'm just someone who has used meditation to end a lot of suffering that my own mind was creating by training and conditioning it to stay in the present moment and the 'reality of what is'.

Before meditation, my untrained mind would constantly bounce between the past and future, or the 'reality of what should, could, or would ideally be happening', which, if you think about it, isn't reality at all.

Reliving and dwelling on past experiences only served to create a depressive state, whereas imagining and projecting what the future would potentially be shifted me into a state of anxiety and dread, both equally as unpleasant and debilitating as the other. Whether ruminating on the past or creating illusions about the future, I wasn't in the driver's seat making executive decisions on which direction I was going in life or how I felt on any given day.

In my daily interactions with people who are curious about meditation, I've found there to be much confusion about what meditation actually is. My goal then in writing this is to make it easier for people to practise meditation by removing the barriers (lack of knowledge and misunderstanding) and simplifying what meditation is.

There are many forms of meditation and ways to create inner peace, including staring at a candle, chanting, repeating a mantra, or the most common way – focusing on breath. The practice I learnt and now share with clients is in the tradition of vipassana meditation, 'vipassana' meaning, "To see things as they are," clearly and objectively. This is achieved by sitting in an upright position with legs crossed, setting an intention to not move for the duration of the meditation, then observing and noticing the thoughts and feelings that arise while in that position. The goal is to neither mindlessly move into a more comfortable position nor let the mind wander off and get lost in thinking about what happened earlier that day or what's for dinner that night.

When we do this consistently, as a natural occurrence, we cultivate a mind that's much more calm, peaceful, and genuinely happy. The lack of internal noise is deafening!

I find it helpful to talk to people about mental health as we do with physical health. We can see the body, so it's more relatable and easier to understand than invisible thoughts and feelings. With that said, meditation or training the mind is a proactive way of keeping the mind healthy and in shape, exactly the same as going to the gym and exercising the body. The body becomes healthier, more resilient, and functions better when we deliberately put it in an environment where it will be under a healthy degree of stress – meditation is no different. Both the mind and body are strengthened through meeting resistance; we just need to learn how to respond in a way that's constructive when we do come into contact with that resistance. This can happen by choice in meditative practice or not by choice in our daily lives when we don't get what we want, people say unpleasant things about us, or we don't have the perfect day. Either way, there are an abundance of opportunities to train your mind and improve your mental health on a daily basis.

Like going to the gym, you can dedicate time each day to meditate, or you can wait until your boss/kids/partner/others do or say something that triggers you and then 'do the work', as we say. My recommendation is that you do both. It's worth mentioning that there's a major difference between feeling stressed and using stress. If you're feeling stressed, there's a high chance you're not using stress to your advantage.

As I mentioned earlier, there's much confusion when it comes to meditation, so, to help clarify it, let's think of the mind as a puppy. The aim of meditation is to train the puppy to sit still rather than running off and chewing your favourite shoes, which you then feel angry or upset about. When I ask clients if they meditate, common answers are, "Yes, I like to listen to guided relaxation" or, "I sometimes contemplate things." Both of these are beneficial but aren't meditation as we know it.

Guided relaxation helps us feel nice. It's enjoyable because it helps reduce stress and tension from the mind and body, which is healthy, but you're not actively involved in the process, so, fundamentally, you aren't achieving any gains in terms of strength and resilience.

Contemplation is great. Some of my best ideas come when I'm in the shower or gardening or just before sleep because I'm not in my analytical mind; I'm just 'being'. In the past, however, if something has affected me and I haven't processed it, in the shower, garden, or bed is where my mind would wander down some deep and dark rabbit holes in which I would get stuck for days or even weeks.

Using the puppy metaphor, I'll help you see the difference between relaxation, contemplation, and meditation so you can make a conscious decision to spend time doing one or more.

- Relaxation – like getting a massage, letting the puppy rest, recover, and feel good
- Contemplation – like stretching, letting the puppy wander but not into dangerous places
- Meditation – like going to the gym, teaching the puppy to sit

All three are valuable and have their place. However, as you meditate more, you'll find you'll need less guided relaxation due to not creating as much stress and tension that needs releasing.

Finally, I would like to elaborate on something I spoke of earlier, and that is 'doing the work' on a daily basis. I encourage people to create a meditative practice of sitting in stillness each day, but I strongly advocate for you to live a meditative life. Sitting on the mat, observing the breath, then watching thoughts and feelings come and go is wonderful, but too many people then open their eyes and get swept up in their days, reacting to everything that happens and finding themselves feeling angry, guilty, depressed, or anxious (or in suffering, as we call it).

What I offer is that we can observe all of the phenomena in the external world just as we do the internal world. It's like training for a sport then never playing a game. Sure, you get better and develop your skills and ability, but it's done in a controlled environment, with coaches directing everyone, and all your team mates are on the same page as you. It's not real life! Real life is where shit hits the fan; people fuck you over; you get fired; your partner cheats on you; your dog dies; you get cancer… Life happens, and you can't control any of it. You can, however, with dedication and patience, learn to control how you feel about all of it.

> I won't sugar-coat it – it's far from easy, but it's totally worth it. And if I can do it, and Shane can do it, and millions of other people can do it, you can do it too.
>
> I wish you all well on your journeys, and I hope I have achieved my goal of making things a bit easier to understand so you can either begin to form a relationship with meditation or strengthen whatever practice you currently have.
>
> Just don't forget to play the game.

DIVERSE MANAGEMENT STRATEGIES – ONE THING CAN'T BE YOUR EVERYTHING

One thing or coping mechanism can't be your everything because it can be stripped away – then what do you have?

As I mentioned early, in 2016 and 2017, I had two surgeries. I'd been training for a 50-kilometre ultramarathon in the Blue Mountains and during one training session, I started getting sharp pains down my hips. I'd done 30 kilometres, which meant I had to walk back 30 kilometres. At that point, I was just done. My body couldn't cope with it, so I took a week off.

The next week, I ran 100 metres, and it was all I could do. I got my hips checked out and had to get surgery. All of a sudden, running, my most important coping mechanism, was gone.

A couple of months later, I met Alicia. On our first date, we walked three or four kilometres along the beach, and my hips were in agony. I didn't tell her at the time, but I knew she was going to become so important to me, so I pushed through the pain.

> ## Lifesaver #5 – Sometimes you need a professional
>
> Along the journey, I've had multiple psychologists or psychotherapists help. Without them, I simply wouldn't be here today. It's a tough thing to reach out and ask for help, especially when some of the best professionals have waiting lists. It's a part of the journey that's necessary in so many cases, and I want to thank those who helped guide, empower, and educate me along the way.
>
> I've been able to learn so much that leads me to live a much healthier lifestyle. Since walking into the mental health clinic, I've had some of the best therapists I could ask for. Ryan, from the Centre for Healing, was there at a really critical stage of my health journey, helping me to understand a lot of my core beliefs, and he connected me to Nick from MyndFit, who has really guided me to a different way of seeing the world around me and within me. In more recent times, I met Tenille, who has also helped me.
>
> All three of these amazing humans have sat with me in the trenches and given me the space I needed so I could climb out again. They're a combined part of the team of lifesavers that help me when I ask.

The biggest lesson I learnt during that period was that you can't only rely on one thing to cope. One thing can't be your everything. It can be stripped away in an instant, no matter what it is, no matter who you are. It's hard to think about this stuff, but I could be in an accident and not be able to exercise or work, or something terrible could happen to my loved ones, and I'd be fucked.

I guess this comes back to using dependent relationships as coping mechanisms. We can't be dependent on them. I had to learn to not be dependent on running anymore and incorporate many different coping strategies. Running is my zone; it's where I go; it's what I do. I put my earphones in, and I go. When I didn't have that, I had to find other things, like the gym. I'm trying to start running again now, and it's interesting what my back and knee are allowing, but I still make sure I have a balance of things. If it's not running, it might be going to the gym. If it's not going to the gym, it's journalling. If it's not journalling, it's meditation. If it's not that, it's putting my phone away and rolling around on the ground with my kids. Honestly, sometimes it's just scrolling through Instagram or Facebook.

The most important thing about any management strategy is to be aware of what you're doing, so, for example, you're not just mindlessly scrolling on your phone until 3 am. Personally, I set a time limit on how much I use my phone as a coping strategy, and it allows me to feel okay for that amount of time. It's all about having that balance and diversity in what you do to help yourself.

IT'S ME LOOKING AFTER ME

I'm really passionate about sport, and one of my management strategies is watching sport – I love cricket and footy. I'd love to work in sport because I could sit there and watch for eight hours and get paid half of what I make now, no issues. I'll sit there and watch eight hours of cricket, and my family is like, "How do you do that?"

"It's my zone. It's me relaxing. It's me switching off. It's me looking after me."

That's part of me looking after my mental health. If I'm not watching sport, you should probably be worried. When things aren't going well for me, it's obvious because I have no interest in the things that are important to me.

Again, it's about finding that balance between healthy and unhealthy. Before we had kids, I used to get up at 4 am and watch the games that were being played in other countries. Now I need to get up for my kids, and I can't get up at 4 am and be tired because I need to look after them. So, now I watch sport after they go to bed or find other times that work for all of us. It's about finding that balance and making sure the rest of your life isn't being affected.

This comes back to my running. It's starting to affect my life because my back pain is affecting my sleeping, and my foot is affecting me when I'm walking around at work. So, this may mean that once I get through this period and reach my goal, I have to give it up, and that's fine. I understand that as we get older, our balance and priorities in our lives change, we manage differently, and that's just the way it is. But I'm not going to give up on running without seeing the experts, so I'm seeing a physio and a podiatrist to try and work it out. However, I accept that things might change and that's how life is.

THE MOST IMPORTANT LIST YOU'LL EVER WRITE

I've found that having a list or page full of things you can do for your mental health is so important. This list shouldn't be a 'top ten'; it should be everything you can think of that really helps you be mindful, makes you feel at home, and helps you de-stress. This list might include things like meditation, having fun with your family, sleep, nutrition (like making sure the right foods are available), seeing friends, and playing with your pets.

Also, don't be perfect. No one can be perfect, and putting pressure on ourselves to be perfect is unhelpful and unhealthy. Another unhealthy approach is doing things out of fear or anxiety. If those are your motivators, it's not actually going to help. As I said earlier about one thing not being your everything, it's also important to do everything in moderation, have balance, and do things mindfully.

This list will change with your life circumstances. For example, my management strategies changed when I had kids because my life and routine changed. So, you'll need to set aside time for these activities and strategies, and do it mindfully. Don't fall into the 'too busy' trap. When we're busy and life gets intense, it's easy to squeeze out the things we love and make us happy because other things get in the way. We stop doing these things because life gets demanding, but that's the trap we shouldn't fall into. It's not hard to do these things, and they have so many benefits, but we do need to consciously do them. Life isn't demanding enough to not prioritise our mental health or focus on the beauty and joy of life.

When I first wrote my list, it had at least 40 things on it that I could do to help my mental health. At the time, I was sitting in my recliner, recovering from two hip operations, and I bought a kitten because she brought me joy and kept me company, allowing me to be mindful and in the moment. Then we had our first child; Alicia's mum passed away, and we adopted her dog. Her dog would have killed the cat, so we gave her away. It wasn't easy to give up something that really helped me in a difficult time, but it wasn't about me in that situation. Alicia losing her mum was a lot more significant than what I was going through, so we prioritised what was important for her and us as a family.

My list also includes reading, and recording podcasts, because these things make me feel good. Podcasts make me feel good because I get to open up about stuff and help other people open up and heal too, and that's fulfilling for me. Writing this book feels good to me too. I work hard to have so many different outlets that help me.

You can separate your list into things that cost money and things that are free so you have space to do both. I love the idea of separating it this way because everybody, regardless of their financial situation, needs to dedicate time to their mental health.

Being able to have your list in your physical space is a good reminder when you're feeling shit, because all the things you can do to help yourself are right there. Us all working on our mental health is already making the world a healthier place to be.

This list is so personal, but there are many universal things that can help mental health, so I've added mine here and given you space to write yours too. I split my list into two sections: what's free and what costs money, so I never have an excuse.

Shane's list:
- Reading
- Journalling
- Family time
- Acts of kindness
- Checking in with someone else

Suggestions:
- Going for a walk
- Seeing friends
- Listening to podcasts
- Calling interstate/overseas friends
- Going for a picnic
- Meditation
- Seeing a therapist
- Reading to the kids
- Board games

- Hiking
- Running
- Having a bath
- Nature – watching a sunset, going to the beach
- _____
- _____
- _____
- _____
- _____
- _____
- _____
- _____
- _____
- _____
- _____

LIVE YOUR LIST

As with everything, living your list is all about balance. Doing these things too much or giving them too much focus at the detriment of other important parts of life can get really unhealthy. Again, if you're doing it out of fear or anxiety, it's not actually helpful. It's probably going to create more suffering in that space for you.

I talked to a friend, Scott, recently on my podcast (episode: Scott Rowe – Travel & Mental Health), who I hadn't seen in ten years. We were catching up about life, and he told me about how he and his girlfriend sold their apartment and everything they owned and bought one-way tickets to Sri Lanka. They travelled the world for a few months, and he wanted to talk about it, focusing on the things that truly make us happy in life.

We know each other from footy, through juniors and the start of our seniors journey. Scott has played footy for quite a few teams, and we were talking about how we've both seen so many men dedicate themselves to sport and drinking culture. He got to a point where he wanted to let go and just leave that environment, and that was okay. He knew it would be there if he wanted to come back to it, but he wanted a change. It's so easy for us to get caught up in whatever is going on and whatever circumstances we're in, and we forget about the things that make us happy. We talked about how we've matured a lot since we were 20, so we can't look at those young men and judge what they're doing, but we can try to help open their eyes to this other world.

Now, every Sunday, Scott goes hiking and fishing, and he just *lives*. He said, "I've never been as happy as I am now. Just living and just being." It's so inspiring to see people not just resting on their laurels but really making what makes them happy happen in their lives. He's truly living his list and is so happy to be happy.

MINDFULNESS AND SLEEP

Mindfulness is also really important for me. One of my early therapists gave me a strategy for calming down or going to sleep: counting down from 99 to 0 in my head. I used to do a lot of these mental countdowns, and I got into the habit early on in adulthood. There have been so many times when I've gotten to zero and had to start again, but now it's ingrained in me. It helped me so much, so it means a lot to me, and I still use it. Sometimes I'll fall asleep before I get to 60, and sometimes I'll realise 15 minutes have gone by and I've stopped counting without noticing. Sometimes I'll drift off a little bit then wake up again and start the countdown at the last number I remember. This is a form of mindfulness, and, for me, it's so helpful before bed. I love this because it's simple and helps me switch off my overthinking mind.

It's important for me to do because, as I've mentioned, nightmares and sleeping issues have caused major problems with my quantity and quality of sleep since primary school. I'm learning so much more about sleep, but, quite often, I still lay awake for hours, and the effect of this is quite scary, as my mind can start to slip into suicidal thought patterns again in the days following.

Meet yourself where you're at with mindfulness and meditation. Do what feels good for you, and don't overwhelm yourself – but do the work.

WHILE FOCUSING ON THE MENTAL, DON'T NEGLECT THE PHYSICAL

Keeping yourself in a good physical space, with exercise and nutrition, also helps keep you in a good emotional and mental space. I want to talk about nutrition here because it plays a big part in our overall health.

I had what would probably be classed as eating issues as a teenager, and I didn't have awareness around that until the last couple of years. Then it went the other way.

I had mentors who would say, "Don't be perfect," but their coaching level made it feel like nothing was ever good enough. I was at a point where I had a six pack. I was so ripped, and I felt so muscly and looked good, but I was extremely burnt out. It was part of the reason why I relapsed. So, the nutrition element is important, but not if you're beating yourself up about it. It's just about eating things that make you feel good, inside and out.

That's where I'm at now as a PT. I've got all this conditioning from what I've been taught, and I'm trying to formulate the knowledge I've been given and what I've gone through myself into something that works for people, because everyone's different. Some people are wired to go all-in and be fine with it, and some people need to be cautious and mindful with it. With my mental health and where I'm at, I just set myself up for success and try to eat the best I can.

I'm still working on it and coming back from a bad place, but the main thing for me is making sure the right foods that make me feel good are readily available. If I eat other things occasionally, then so be it. I know I'm not living extremely unhealthily. I don't want to reach any fitness or nutrition goals by being really hard on myself and trying to be perfect. I want to do it by just living the life I want to live.

So, it's about not stressing about it. We do meal prep in our home, and I'll try to keep it as basic as I can at the moment because living so busily makes it difficult. If I can pull back a bit on work hours at some stage in the future, I'd love to do a lot more meal prep and make some better meals too. Currently, one of our aims is to have the kids help with this kind of stuff, because we want them to be really involved in making different healthy dishes as they grow up so they can learn these skills. It's not what we grew up with, and we think it's really valuable going forward.

So, making sure I'm eating as healthily as possible – without mentally beating myself up about it – and having it planned out as much as I can is important for me. I also know that plans aren't always going to work out because life does happen, so it's important to be as prepared as possible.

It's also important to not be hard on yourself when plans don't work out. You might be struggling and can't cook, or the food you have doesn't feel good for you in that moment, and eating it would make you feel like shit. In these situations, it's easier and often mentally more helpful and healthy to get something you'll enjoy, regardless of what it is.

Aiming for perfection around eating is unhealthy. Everything is okay in moderation, and binge eating is a lot worse for you than moderation and just eating intuitively. If every now and then you want something 'unhealthy', that's okay. You can eat it in moderation and not binge, and it's a really nice experience to just enjoy the food you like.

On the day I'm writing this, we have a food delivery coming, and there are lots of good veggies, meats, and fruits in there, but there's also ice cream, and I'm excited about it. My plan for this week is to eat really well, and we haven't had ice cream in ages, so I'm excited to sit on the couch with Alicia, enjoy a movie, and eat ice cream together. It's all about us doing and experiencing that together. Moderation is okay.

DAILY ROUTINE TABLE

Instead of putting a lot of pressure on myself these days, I just aim to be the best version of myself each day, and creating a daily routine is one of the simplest ways for me to achieve that. I've learnt that goals are important, but, throughout life, I've got so caught up in them, which leads to complete overwhelm. Overwhelm for someone who has a fallback of crippling anxiety, depression, and suicidal tendencies isn't a good recipe for success.

In setting goals, I understand they can't be expectations, and I understand I may never reach some goals, but that doesn't mean I don't try.

My daily routine is key for me, and I keep it simple, allowing the focus to be on only the next step. There's a scene I love from the book *The Boy, the Mole, the Fox and the Horse* by Charlie Mackesy:

"I can't see a way through," said the boy.

"Can you see your next step?"

"Yes."

"Just take that," said the horse.[1]

---

[1] Mackesy, C 2019, *The Boy, the Mole, the Fox and the Horse*, Ebury Digital.

The key for me and for many others who experience mental distress is to only focus on the next step, allowing ourselves to be in the moment, where nothing else matters.

Here's a basic table you may want to use as a guide or for some accountability. You can change it to reflect what you want your daily routine to look like.

Date:	
Awake/up:	
Bed/sleep:	
Study and work hours:	
Reading:	
Walk:	
Stretches:	
Training:	

EVERYONE'S DEALING WITH THEIR OWN SHIT

I was recording a podcast with my friend, Scott, recently, and he said, "I don't know if you remember this…"

Where's this going? I thought, knowing I probably wouldn't remember.

Scott said he just wanted to apologise because, one day when we were 19, I turned up at the footy club, and he said something along the lines of, "Come on, mate, you need to stop doing shit like that." Of course, he was talking about my behaviour when I was in a really bad place, and he wanted to apologise now because, at the time, he didn't understand what I was going through. However, through listening to my podcast and me sharing my story, he finally understood. He didn't realise at the time because all he saw were some Facebook posts that he thought were attention seeking, but, really, I was looking for help.

I appreciated the apology, even though I didn't remember the incident, but it made me think about how many other people had said those kinds of things to me. Usually, I just blew them off, but they did affect me. I was likely feeling that way within myself, and what people said reinforced what I was already thinking. I said that to him. I probably didn't think too much about it because I already believed it anyway. He said that ever since he started listening to my podcast, he felt like he needed to apologise for it, and it hadn't left his mind. I really appreciated it because it reinforced that this book will open people's eyes. If someone reads it, someone who maybe said something similar years ago to a friend who was struggling, it might encourage them to reach out, apologise, check in, and clear the air.

It nearly made me cry when he told me because we've always been mates, and it never affected our friendship. We were both ignorant. Unfortunately, that's often the way it is. People don't know about mental health, and they say things because they're ignorant, through no fault of their own.

It takes a good person to own that sort of stuff and when we know better, we do better. That's what I want from this book – I want to help people know and do better. I don't think there's a human being who hasn't become more aware of a particular subject or phenomenon in the world and not reconsidered how they've acted about it in the past, and thought about how to change in the future. As we grow and heal and learn, we become different people, and it's important to acknowledge that we can only do what we can with the consciousness and knowledge we've got at the time. We often get so caught up in our own lives that we forget people are going through their own shit and have entire lives that we don't think or know about.

What Scott said to me was he's learnt that we're all here on this earth with things in our lives, and we don't know what's going on for other people. Someone might try to help in the only way they know how, and it might be the wrong way, but they're trying. The great thing is that they learn. We can all learn how to support people in better ways, and we can all find people who support our mental health in healthy ways.

OWNING IT – THE REMEDY TO SHAME

When it comes to our mental health, sometimes we can feel ashamed – of our behaviour, of our struggles, of not being able to cope. Shame is where a lot of mental health issues and unnecessary suffering stem from. It can feel scary to be vulnerable and to expose that shame or even label and communicate it, but talking about it is the very thing that liberates us.

When I feel ashamed, it's usually because I feel I've gone outside the parameters of my values and beliefs. If I'm living within my values and beliefs, I don't feel much real shame. So, when we go outside our own values, that's generally when shame starts to creep in. For a long time, I dealt with this very unhealthily, through burying, ignoring, suppressing, and avoiding it. Now, it's about owning it and saying, "Yes, I did this, and it wasn't in my values and beliefs." If that means someone else needs to set a boundary, then that's okay. It might hurt, but the reality is if you don't own it, it will sit with you anyway, and that will play out somehow.

I've made some massive mistakes in the past – frankly, I still make them now – but the difference is that I own each and every single one of them when I'm aware of them. It's easy to get carried away sometimes. For instance, I might go out drinking with the boys and end up having a few too many. The next day, I own it. I apologise to whoever needs to hear it, and I try to learn from my mistakes and not let it happen again. But we all get carried away from time to time and when we do, it's the ego at play. We're not being true to ourselves. Once we accept that we're not perfect and never will be, sitting down and having those conversations, discussing our mistakes, gets easier, and the shame quickly fades. We must be accountable for our actions. We must be accountable to ourselves. We must own it.

When we set clear boundaries for ourselves, it's easy to see when we've crossed the line. For example, Alicia doesn't like drug use so when Ryder was born, I put a stop to it. However, one day when she was away with the kids, I used. The next day, I was lying in bed, hungover, vomiting, and consumed with guilt and shame. I knew I'd crossed the line, so I called Alicia and told her what had happened. I explained that I knew she'd be angry and disappointed in me and next time I felt like I might slip, I'd leave with her instead of staying at home.

So, by accepting the situation, my actions, my slip-up, I learnt from the experience, and we were both able to move on in a positive way. There are always going to be consequences, and we should accept those too. The guilt and the shame don't need to be all-consuming. Instead, they can guide us to make decisions that better align with our values.

Anyone who knows me well knows that I'm my own harshest critic. If I do something that doesn't fall within my values or beliefs, I can be really hard on myself. But by owning those mistakes and having those honest conversations, I'm able to keep moving forward. I don't get bogged down, dwelling on whatever punishment I think I deserve. Most people appreciate the honesty, even if they're angry and disappointed at first.

Once you realise that you can move forward in a positive way, it makes going into future situations easier. It relieves a lot of the external pressure to be perfect and removes much of the anxiety that can make rationally dealing with the situation difficult. When we're highly emotional, we make poor decisions. It's a fact. So, by owning our actions in a rational and honest way, we avoid the knee-jerk emotional reaction that often makes a bad situation worse.

Let your values and beliefs be your guide. If we were all true to our values and beliefs most of the time, we'd live in a pretty friendly society. Of that, I'm sure.

ACCOUNTABILITY AND COMMUNICATION

Part of my mental health work has been learning to accept that I'm not perfect, and another part is being accountable. Being accountable involves not resting on your laurels, actually learning from your mistakes, and making changes.

It's important to be accountable to the people around you, as well as being accountable to yourself, and letting them know what's going on in your life. Sometimes, we don't know how to speak to each other. But it's important that we learn because in order to tell people what's going on, we need to be able to communicate in healthy and productive ways.

As I became an 'adult' and started doing adult things, like getting a job, getting into serious relationships, playing at sporting clubs, and having kids, I realised I was missing a key ingredient to functioning with other adults in a healthy manner – healthy and honest conversations.

For decades, I took a reactive rather than a proactive approach to life. I was reacting to situations instead of preparing for them. However, by getting proactive and learning to regulate my emotions and have healthy conversations, I gained the ability to build healthy, strong relationships with others and also myself.

I've mentioned Matt Runnalls' work before, and I'm sure I'll mention it again, but I love supporting what he does. At Mindfull Aus, he's giving kids important skills I'm now learning in my thirties. I wish I'd learnt about accountability and communication sooner.

NECESSARY VS. UNNECESSARY SUFFERING

In my journey, I've learnt about necessary versus unnecessary suffering. Nick taught me a lot of this stuff and has helped me put it into words and describe it. So, what is necessary versus unnecessary suffering? Let me explain.

If you do something outside of your values and beliefs, there's going to be some necessary suffering around that. You're going to be upset and disappointed and maybe feel shame, but don't let it spiral. Don't get angry and disappointed at those feelings. Cut the cord so you don't spiral into unnecessary suffering.

As part of this, I've learnt we can't pile it on. Don't get angry at your anger or your other feelings, because that's not helpful or healthy. That's unnecessary suffering that you're putting yourself through. While we need to be self-aware, we can't punish ourselves. We need to take it easy on ourselves. We need to be gentle.

Like I said, there's necessary suffering and unnecessary suffering, and you need to make a choice to not spiral into the unnecessary type. Instead, you can find healthy ways to get through the necessary suffering.

When both Ryder and Alicia's mum were in hospital in 2021, I was a wreck. When I talked to Nick about it, he helped me realise I was going through necessary suffering and said he'd be more worried if I wasn't struggling because that would be denial and repression, and those reactions would cause more issues down the track. If you're not suffering in situations like that, that's a problem. We're all humans who are going to experience terrible things – we're going to struggle – but we will get through it and be okay.

When a loved one passes away, we're allowed to grieve and be sad and angry, but don't pile it on. Don't get angry at yourself because you've sat there crying for three hours. That's normal, natural, and okay. You need to process it and work through it.

Many mental health challenges are the result of unnecessary suffering because we pile on all these extra negative feelings. However, we can work through all of that. We can work against the unnecessary suffering.

CATCH THE THOUGHT

At MyndFit, Nick taught me a really great mental prep strategy to work through the necessary suffering and avoid the unnecessary suffering. I call it 'catch the thought'. This exercise treats certain thoughts like a train that has left the station without a driver, and it's about stopping that train in its tracks instead of letting it go faster and faster.

The first step of any mental health work is awareness, so you have to learn to be aware of your thoughts and determine which are there to think through and which are there to catch.

There are four steps to this exercise:
1. Catch
2. Laugh
3. Rewind
4. Step back

The first step, **catch**, is about gently stopping the train (the thought) that has left the station. That thought is running away from you, and catching it allows you to start taking back control so you can start transitioning back to the present moment.

At the second step, it's time to **laugh** at the thought. Look at the thought and realise how silly it is. It's not reality; it's not logic; it's just a thought you don't need. Unnecessary suffering, judgement, and blame are silly, and we don't need them. Those thoughts are irrational. They're based on previous trauma or mental health challenges, and they're there to work through but not listen to. If you have the ability to laugh or smile or chuckle at these thoughts, the situation changes. You start to experience positive feelings instead of focusing on the negative, irrational thoughts.

The third step is to **rewind** and bring the train (thought) back to the station mindfully. Personally, I picture a train leaving my mind, and I need to put it back in its train yard because it wasn't time for it to leave. No driver = no leaving the station.

Lastly, it's important to take a **step back**. Getting a bit of distance from the thought instead of giving in to it, getting caught up in it, and spiralling is essential. I can observe the thought with distance, logic, and objectiveness. I can see it much more clearly because it's not necessarily embedded in my whole system.

The more I practise this exercise, the better I get. It's essentially being mindful about what I'm doing and thinking day to day. It's a pretty simple tool that you can do anywhere, anytime. It's about the more mindful practice of examining and working through thoughts. It's an exercise to short-circuit your brain and your nervous system. It allows you to rewind back into reality and realise it was just a thought – it's not rational, and it's not true. Then you can go down a more constructive path.

The thoughts that run through our minds aren't the centrepieces of who we are. The deeper our attachment to these thoughts, the deeper our suffering is. So, it's about learning to let go and focus on reality, what the situation actually needs, and what you need in that situation. You want your attachment to be healthy and any suffering you experience to be necessary, not unnecessary. We need to have healthy relationships with our struggles.

SETTING BOUNDARIES FOR EVERYONE'S BENEFIT

I really care about people, and I love helping others, which is why I do what I do, but it can be emotionally draining to care and worry so much about other people, so it's important for us all to take care of ourselves while helping others. A really important part of taking care of ourselves is setting boundaries.

Boundaries all depend on you, who you are, what you want, and your circumstances. My boundaries really depend on my life circumstances. They were pretty wide open when I wasn't married and didn't have kids, but now I have to set more boundaries so I have the time and emotional energy for my family. That's reality.

Boundaries also depend on the person you're setting the boundary with because it depends on how that relationship actually affects you. If a relationship gets to a point where it's unhealthy, you need to set a boundary for yourself, not just for the other person. When we're attached to someone, their struggles really matter to us, which can be a problem in some cases. As I mentioned earlier, when I was a teenager and relied on girls to help my mental health instead of helping myself, those girls putting boundaries in place was scary for them and for me, but so necessary and healthy.

Here's one of the rawest examples I recall…

In 2013, I started seeing someone. Her name was Eliza, and the relationship was going great until I had one of those nights when I thought alcohol could help me through a mental health battle. After a night full of drinking, I turned up at Eliza's house, uninvited and unwelcomed. Thankfully, I was also ignored, being left outside in the rain. I knew word was getting around that I was standing outside her house, knocking on her door, because people who knew us both were calling me, but I ignored their calls.

At the time, I was already suicidal, clutching to the idea that she would make me feel better. I'd been down that road many times before, having girls around to try and help me feel mentally better, but it never worked. Why would it this time? An irrational, unhealthy, and unstable mind, with alcohol thrown in the mix, didn't allow for great decisions.

More people started calling and texting, trying to find out what was happening, so I took off. I recognised that going to Eliza's house wasn't right. Now, on top of being suicidal, I was ashamed and full of guilt, as word spread that I was threatening suicide again.

In a moment of recognising I didn't want to die – I just wanted all those shitty feelings to go away – I agreed to let someone come and pick me up. *How can anyone forgive me this time?* I thought, as the shame set deeper and deeper.

In the end, forgiveness was delivered by those closest to me, but they set a clear boundary. My actions and behaviour wouldn't be tolerated, and I had to respect Eliza's wishes to never speak to her again. Essentially, I had to learn that what I did wasn't on.

Fuck, what a screw up, I thought as I entered my own pity party. However, compared to other pity parties I'd found myself at previously, this one was treated differently by the people around me. Friends didn't go easy on me this time, admitting they could no longer stand by me if I kept behaving the way I did.

While reality was hard, in hindsight, Eliza and my closest friends provoked one of the biggest shifts in my mindset, and their boundaries taught me a lot of what I implement today. As another relationship ended, I realised if I didn't make changes, my dream of being a dad would slip further and further away, as would some of my best friends. I had to change, and only I could make those changes. Those changes needed to be for me, not for others, which my friends respectfully told me.

Now I think about boundaries a lot and put them in place for myself. Over the years, many people have come to me about their mental health, and, for so long, I rode the waves with them. I had no boundaries because I wanted to do whatever I could to help them get better. Then I reached a point in 2020 where I couldn't do it anymore. I had all these people's problems in my head, weighing on me, and I realised I couldn't allow that if I wanted to be a healthy father and husband. Now I've found a way to enforce boundaries, and it really works for me. I'll only allow people to come to me about something three times. If they don't implement anything or do anything to help themselves, I suggest that they find someone else to help them. That might sound cruel, but I care about myself enough to not let people walk all over me, and I can't just blindly support and help someone when they're not helping themselves.

I've had people come to me repeatedly for a couple of years about the same stuff over and over and over again. Every time, we'd have the same chat, and I'd try to give advice about what they could do and what would help. Whenever I asked if they'd tried the strategy or solution I'd suggested, the answer was always no. I came to the realisation that I wasn't even helping these people anymore. Instead, I was enabling more of this behaviour.

This all came down to one question: what is my worth? After all I've done to grow and heal and work on myself, I finally feel like I'm worthy. Previously, I didn't think I was worthy of time and money, and there was this huge lack of self-worth and self-confidence in who I was. During that period, I was offering a lot of advice that I wasn't taking on myself. I didn't have my shit together, and I still don't in some ways, but I've started taking my own advice and making changes for the better, including setting boundaries.

I think it's one of the most important skills. Whether we call it a skill or not, setting boundaries is essential. We have to do it. I'll never stop doing what I'm doing, discussing mental health, and people are going to set boundaries around that. They might not want to hear it, be around it, or be involved in it. Because of this, they're going to set boundaries, and both the 'giver' and 'receiver' of the boundary need to accept that. It doesn't mean it doesn't hurt, because it does, but both people need to look after themselves. So, it always has to come back to two questions: *Am I healthy? How am I looking after myself?*

IT'S ON YOU

Blaming someone for your anxiety, your stress, or your depression just can't happen. The anxiety, stress, and depression are your reactions, and yours alone, to what has happened. When you blame someone else, a few things occur:

1. You empower someone else with your feelings and thoughts. This is unhealthy because many of these people can't control their own feelings and thoughts, let alone yours.
2. You lose power and control instantly, along with the ability to handle the situation in a healthy manner.
3. You simply won't be happy (or happiness in life will be very fleeting) because you're outsourcing happiness rather than finding it within.

It's important to take your power back – empower yourself, and happiness will be intrinsic.

In the midst of a storm, or when recalling traumatic events in your life, it's so easy to lay blame on someone else, something else, or even yourself. For years, it was never my fault, or it was *all* my fault. This all changed when I wanted to take control, and I started to only focus on what I could control. I examined what my responsibility was, which allowed me to heal, process, and take steps forward for my own wellbeing, rather than going backwards.

DO IT FOR YOU, DO IT FOR THOSE AROUND YOU

The original PSV journal was founded during the most challenging time of my life. During my journey, I attempted to take my own life, admitted myself to a mental health clinic, and suffered internal bleeding when my kidney was torn playing footy, but none of that compared to the challenges I was about to face.

On 3 April 2021, I married the love of my life, and we were aiming to set our life up over the next 12 weeks before we welcomed our first son into the world. After a short trip away, our family dog, Jett, passed away suddenly, which rocked us. Before we even had a chance to grieve the loss, Alicia went into labour, and our son was born ten weeks premature. Due to the COVID-19 pandemic, we were unable to have the full support and love of our loved ones as we began this part of our journey. Then there was the impact COVID had on our businesses. We pushed all of that aside quickly because, ultimately, we had a job to do – to be there for our son, who was fighting for his life in the Mercy Hospital for Women.

During this time, the support of family and friends was extremely important, and it was getting us through the challenges that a premature baby brings. Then, 18 days later, Alicia got the call to say her mum was being rushed to hospital. Alicia's dad had passed away from cancer nine years prior, and we were so worried. With Alicia's mum in Maroondah and Ryder in the Mercy, we sat up awake that night, not knowing what would happen. We'd already been in fight-or-flight mode with the phone calls from the Mercy, and we now had another hospital that would be calling us.

At 4 am, with us on less than two hours sleep, the phone rang, and we heard words we never expected to hear, as Alicia's mum was a bloody tough and healthy woman: "Your mum is bleeding from the brain and will be transferred to St Vincent's now."

We'd spent 18 days in one hospital and for the next 40, we split our time between two hospitals – one with our son, fighting at the start of his life, and one with my mother-in-law, fighting at what turned out to be the end of hers. In 58 days, we saw a neonatal intensive care unit, an adults' intensive care unit, a stroke unit, and palliative care every single day. The challenge to stay afloat through this was the biggest of my life.

I made it a priority each day to make sure I did three things for my health so I could give the best of myself to my family during this time. Trust me – I broke down. I cried every second day. But I'd hate to think what would've happened if I didn't look after myself. I stood by my wife, my son, and my mother-in-law in what felt like one crazy TV show.

Those 58 days changed our world but if I hadn't done the hard work on my mental wellbeing in the previous years, there was simply no way I'd still be married today. Previously, when life got difficult, I turned destructive but by reaching out in the years prior, I became the man my family needed and could rely on.

This part of my journey could be its own book, and maybe, one day, it will be. But for now, I want people to understand that we all have storms in our lives, and it's when you walk into them with a strong foundation and solid mental wellbeing that you come out the other side being able to control the controllables. Also, when you're mentally well, you'll get much more enjoyment out of the 'good' times. Doing the work on you changes your world and the world around you.

The original PSV 'Three for Me' journal was created from this challenging period of my life. It got me through and helped me stay out of deep depression. It allowed me to always be there for those who needed me most.

Was the journal my saviour? No. I had great support from friends, and I asked them for help. I also had a great therapist, who explained that, during times like these, it was important to recognise that it wasn't about perfection. It was about doing my best – and I did my best.

This book is made to help others, whether you're going through a tough time or not. It's about bringing your conscious and subconscious minds together to put you first because if you're not putting yourself first enough, you'll burn out, and those around you will never get the best of you. Do it for you, and do it for those around you.

THEY'RE JUST THOUGHTS

> If there is an immediate risk of harm to yourself or others, please call 000 (or the emergency line in your area). You can also call the Suicide Call Back Service on 1300 659 467 or Lifeline on 13 11 14.

In the end, suicidal thoughts are just thoughts. However, when they're continually suppressed and not talked about, they become more of a problem. For someone who isn't experiencing these thoughts and doesn't understand them, it's a really challenging thing to hear. However, when we experience suicidal thoughts, we need to express them so we can deal with them and also let the people around us know how we're feeling so they can help us and we can help ourselves.

In my 20 years of experiencing suicidal thoughts, I've really struggled with the best way to approach talking about them. In 2021, I was working for a mate, doing some landscaping, and, at the time, I was in the best headspace I'd ever been in. Then, one night, out of the blue, I had suicidal nightmares and woke up with suicidal thoughts. Because I'd been in such a great headspace and they came out of nowhere, it completely threw me. I turned off my phone and hid in my room, and I felt so guilty because I couldn't go into work. I just blocked my mate's number. Then I was left sitting there with these suicidal thoughts, the fact I'd let a mate down, missed a day of work, and lost the money I would've earned.

Once before my suicide attempt, a friend said to me, "You get sick so often." But I wasn't always sick physically like I'd told everyone. I'd miss footy or cricket training, or text in sick for work once a week in my late teenage years, because I couldn't call anyone when I was having suicidal thoughts. When I'm having those thoughts, I'm still able to do some things, but one thing I'm unable to do is drive because it's not safe for me. Not being able to drive meant I couldn't get to work.

My logical mind does understand that these thoughts don't control me, and I do know that I won't act on them. I know that these thoughts are trying to tell me something important, so it's crucial I take the lesson from them, rather than letting them take over my life completely. Despite understanding this, suicidal thoughts can be daunting and debilitating, so it's important that the person experiencing them has a safe space to talk about them.

For those who aren't comfortable listening, my message to you is that someone having these thoughts doesn't necessarily mean they're suicidal or are going to act on them, but it is important that they get these thoughts out and acknowledge what's going on so they can start healing. Yes, it's uncomfortable, but, in that moment, please make it all about the other person and not about you. Hug them, listen to them, be there for them.

If someone tells you these deep thoughts, they clearly want you to be there for them. That's a privilege because they're putting trust in you.

For those experiencing suicidal thoughts:

1. Find someone you can be vulnerable with in a safe space.
2. Remind yourself that they're only thoughts, and thoughts don't control you.
3. Remember that wanting the thoughts not to be there or getting angry or frustrated at them won't help. You'll start to enter a cycle and make yourself feel worse.

4. Allow yourself time to work through the thoughts, your feelings, and anything else that may come up.
5. Know that the thoughts will pass in time, as do all thoughts. Thoughts, like everything, have an expiry date.
6. Journal the experience with the new learnings you can take with you if or when it happens again.

From me to you – you are worth it; you are loved, and we want you here!

Also, remember to always seek professional help to get further skills to manage your mental health and suicidal thoughts. Professional help isn't always available in the short-term, so ensure that appointments are booked in advance. Even if you're feeling well at appointment time, it's important to follow through and continue to work on things.

CHAPTER 9

FOR THE CAREGIVERS

CARE FOR THE CAREGIVERS

When taking care of people struggling with mental health, it's important for caregivers to look after themselves too.

My best strategies for caregivers are:

- Be supportive.
- Look after yourself – you can't keep giving.
- Keep the door open.
- Set boundaries and have self-worth and self-respect in maintaining them.
- Make a list of things you can do for yourself.
- Put strategies in place to avoid guilt and burnout.
- Talk about it – see a therapist yourself. Make sure you have someone to go to as well as being there for others.
- Be an example for others – model good mental health behaviours and strategies, especially to people who are struggling.
- Speak to other caregivers, for advice and comfort.

In this section, I'm going to dive a little deeper into these strategies that you may want to try or recommend to someone else.

Be supportive

The first part of helping someone is being supportive. Helping someone is about being a friend and just being there. You don't necessarily have to do something; just being there is doing

> ## Lifesaver #6 – My caregivers
>
> Mental illness can be extremely debilitating for the individual, which means their needs are quite often high. That puts a lot of pressure and potential stress on caregivers. Throughout so many of my darkest days, I had a group of friends and my immediate family who saw me at my absolute worst and, at times, rode the wave of my mental illness with me. They challenged me, supported me, and loved me in each part of the battle.
>
> To you all, and you know who you are, I thank you for being either the physical or mental lifesavers, or sometimes both. I feel like I owe you all so much because I know standing by someone who's struggling with their mind is a challenge.
>
> These lifesavers are the true heroes who put themselves down on their own priority list at the most critical times. Without them, I wouldn't be here today.
>
> They're lifesaver #6 because it's not always a moment but a day-to-day, week-to-week, and even year-to-year proposition to stand directly in the impact zone time and time again.
>
> Thank you, lifesavers.

something. Just being there and being a friend is the most fundamental thing in supporting someone. Sometimes we try to jump to putting all this effort into fixing someone or their situation instead of focusing on the daily support. Often, they don't need or want you to fix it; they just want your friendship and support. They need a friend.

You also need to remember there's a difference between supporting someone and being or feeling responsible for them. Someone's decisions and actions are not in your control, are not your fault, and are not your responsibility.

It's important to remember that every single person is doing the best they can with what they know. Try to see it from all sides and understand where others are coming from – helping and supporting someone is all about empathy.

My friend, Scott, and I talked about support and struggling with helping someone when he came on the podcast. He asked, "What do you do if you're helping someone and you're trying to figure out when it's time to stop?"

My first questions to people asking this are, "What do you like about having that friendship or relationship?" and, "What are the things you do within that relationship to keep the relationship?" I listed around 10 to 12 things that are important in my friendships and relationships, and I asked, "How many people actually do those things with their friends?"

So, ultimately, when you're trying to help someone, you just need to be a friend and do the things on that list. It's not complicated. We often try to fix them, which isn't helpful for you or them, when we should do things from this list of basic human support instead.

Look after yourself – you can't keep giving

For my mum, Alicia, and other people around me, their priorities are themselves, not me. When you're going through mental health issues, that's not what you want to hear, and it's not what your loved ones want to say, but the reality is that they have to. Otherwise, they'll end up in shit too. We all have to give, but we also have to look after ourselves so we can help ourselves and others. There's a reason why on a plane they want you to put your own mask on first, and it's the same in life. Put your own mask on, and you'll be able to help others around you.

Keep the door open

Keep the door open to help someone. Quite often, parents ask me how to help their teenage kids who won't talk to them but clearly have some mental struggles. Keeping the door ajar is one bit of advice, and there's a couple of reasons. Pushing someone to do something often means they end up doing it for the wrong reasons, whereas keeping the door open is about letting the person struggling know you're there. Everything happens on their terms, giving them control and power, which is a big driver for long-term change. This can even be done physically by going to a separate part of the home or building but being ready.

Helping someone is all about understanding them and putting yourself in their shoes. Getting that understanding not only helps them, but it gives you more skills to better help them and also help yourself.

When I think about what I can do to help a friend, it always starts with looking after myself so when they're ready to come to me, the door is ajar. Don't shut that door – just leave it open for when they need it.

Set clear boundaries

It's important to help as much as you can, but also set boundaries to help both yourself and the other person. Particularly when you're around someone who has severe mental health issues, you need to learn about boundaries. We can be pretty shit at boundaries when we love someone and we're trying to help them, but both people in that situation need the boundaries.

Now that I'm working with people with severe and complex mental health issues, one of the things that was drilled into us is that they haven't had boundaries for years or decades of their lives, but we all need them. We need to set boundaries, but we also need to respect boundaries. When someone sets a boundary, it makes it clear that they won't let anyone walk all over them. Some people might not respect your boundaries or try to test them, and it's important to take control and empower yourself to make sure you're keeping those boundaries in place.

Make your own list

In terms of looking after yourself as a caregiver, it can be really helpful to make your own list of things you can do for yourself and your mental health.

Make sure you do things from your list while you're helping someone. Maybe get up earlier than you usually do to go for a walk or journal. Make sure you dedicate time to looking after yourself, and do things from your list regularly. Or if you've had one of those days, look at your list and find something that will help you in that moment. If you've spent the day with your loved one while they've been suicidal, going to the gym is probably not the answer because your body is already under a lot of stress. Instead, find something relaxing that will help your mind. It may be one of those things that are seen as 'unhealthy', like having some ice cream or watching Netflix. However, these things aren't unhealthy if you do them healthily, in moderation. Just make sure that, whatever you're doing, you're putting yourself first and looking after your own mental health.

Talk about it

One thing that's essential is talking about what's going on with people who will listen and support you. At work, when we're working with complex clients, we always debrief and give each other the space (in a confidential way). We're always aware of what's going on and how one another are feeling. When someone walks back in after a tough session, we ask what happened and talk about it for however long they need. We listen.

So, as a caregiver, make sure you have someone to go to as well. If you start bottling it up, you'll end up in a bad headspace too because you're shouldering all of it alone. How many relationships struggle when someone is struggling because, all of a sudden, their partner is struggling too? It can become toxic if it's all bottled up and not dealt with in a healthy way.

I've covered this one a bit because I've talked about how everyone should see a therapist, but this is relevant here too. It comes under caregivers needing to talk to someone themselves but, also, if the person you're supporting asks you about therapy, you can talk to them about how it has helped you.

Many of the people I've spoken too about mental health are caregivers, be it as a parent, spouse, friend, or family member. They aren't paid and don't want to be. They just want to help. When helping someone with mental health issues, you tend to want to protect the person, so you keep it to yourself. This process means you take a lot on but never have your own release. Caregiver fatigue is a real thing, so finding someone you can talk to is crucial for you and the one you're caring for.

Be an example

When someone is struggling with their mental health, they might struggle with having a setback, not being able to set boundaries, or not looking after themselves, and they might not have self-worth or self-confidence. So, you need to be the example. When you're trying to help someone put management strategies or tools for good mental health in place, if you're doing those things for your own mental health, it shows the person who you're helping how they can do it too.

You can also be an example through going to therapy yourself, explaining what you've done and how it has helped you. By doing this, you reduce the stigma. It's such a helpful example to set.

As another example, if you've got a friend struggling and you're starting to struggle, you could ask if they want to come for a walk with you. It's helping them in a way that's practical, and you're doing it together.

I've learnt that leading by example is a great way to teach people. With my son, Ryder, we can't just tell him to do something because he won't do it unless we're doing it too. We teach by example because people repeat what they see and learn what's modelled to them. You may start by letting the person who's struggling know you're going for a walk and say they're welcome to join, and they might not join at first, but they will one day, or they'll do it themselves because they've seen how it has helped you.

Avoiding guilt

I've seen a lot of caregivers struggle with feelings of guilt. There's this stigma that we don't do enough to stop suicide, and there's so much guilt that comes from feeling like we didn't help someone enough, but, as I've said, someone else's mental health isn't your responsibility. You have limited capacity to help someone else's mental health. You can support and help them as much as possible, but their decisions, actions, and thoughts aren't on you – so it's not your guilt to take on either.

There's no way you can fix or help someone's trauma or what they're going through. Every single day, every single human is doing the best they can. You can't argue with someone's trauma – because they're just doing the best they can.

When you hold that mindset – the belief that everyone is just doing the best they can with what they know – you lose the judgement. I think the caregiver who's feeling guilt can apply that same mindset to themselves and say, "I'm doing the best I can. That's enough, and that's okay."

That's as simple as it needs to be. It might not take away the guilt but if a caregiver is feeling a lot of guilt, they probably need to do some work with a therapist because, in reality, a situation that isn't about them might now be consuming them. It's totally okay and normal, but it's something to be aware of for yourself. Guilt, anxiety, and sadness are natural emotions, but, again, unnecessary suffering, like when guilt becomes harmful and unhealthy, is not okay. If it gets to that point, it's time to reach out to someone who can help you, or for the person you're supporting to set that boundary.

If you've lost someone to mental health issues, whether that be through suicide, addiction, or disconnection, here's the reminder that you did the best you could with what you knew.

Avoiding burnout

Working to avoid burnout comes down to what each individual needs to do for themselves. Is this putting yourself first? Is it doing things on your list? Is it seeing a therapist even when you're doing well? All of these things can help prevent burnout, so you can choose what works for you.

Often, burnout can come with dealing with mental health struggles and really emotional topics and experiences. We probably don't talk about this enough because there's such a stigma around it, and you might not want to break the confidence of the person who's sharing their experiences with you, but it is important to talk about what's going on and deal with it to avoid burnout.

Sometimes you can't help, and that's okay

It's okay to say no to helping someone. It's okay to say you're having a hard time with it or it's asking too much of you and suggest other people the person who's been relying on or confiding in you could go to for help.

Recently, someone came to me and said, "I can't be the one who helps my son anymore." Unfortunately, so many of us get to that point when we're helping someone. I don't think any of us want to get to that point, so it's important to keep those boundaries. It's also about trying to empower people, both the caregivers and the people they're caring for, to make the right decisions for themselves. Part of helping someone deal with their mental health is accepting that sometimes you just can't help, which may sound brutal, but it's part of facing the reality of your circumstances. It's okay to say you can't be that person for someone all the time.

One of the challenges for caregivers of people who're struggling with suicidal thoughts or ideation is that we think we can save everyone – but we can't. We don't always have full control over diseases like cancer and heart disease, and we don't have control over mental health either, but, for some reason, it's seen differently. We think we have more control over people's mental health. The reality is that we can't always control everything, and we're not responsible for other people or their health, either physical or mental. We need to set those boundaries and know that someone's actions aren't our fault or responsibility. We can't always help, and that's okay.

Getting support from other caregivers

When I started writing this book, I sat down with my mum and Alicia to talk them through everything that had happened through my eyes so it wasn't a surprise when the book came out. I really went into the depths of what I'd gone through, and I could see Alicia sitting there trying not to cry. She hadn't heard all of the details before. She didn't know the engine was in the passenger seat when I crashed my car, and talking about all of those details was tough, but I needed to be open. I also asked Mum about the nightmares I experienced as a kid because I didn't remember everything. Apparently, I had a lot of nightmares that led to me sleepwalking around the house. Having this chat, all together, was so healing and comforting, and it was beneficial for Mum and Alicia to have each other as supports.

My mum has so much experience with supporting people with mental health challenges. She helped me as much as she could when I was younger, and she has helped family members who struggle too. Mum has seen it all. In the last 12 months, I've only started to truly understand how important everything she did was. She had a real level of understanding of how to help but also set boundaries. Obviously, it was really difficult for her because when it's your own child who's struggling, there's a lot more emotional attachment and difficulty. But she has helped so many people.

Part of writing this book is for her. She'll be one of the first people I hand it to when it's published because she's been so instrumental in supporting me and helping our family get through mental health challenges and learn, heal, and grow.

Caregivers getting support from other caregivers with similar experiences is so beneficial. Before I went to the mental health clinic, Alicia and I talked to several family members. Mum was so supportive and loving, and my aunt, who has been to an inpatient mental health clinic, and uncle were both incredibly helpful. We asked them what it would be like and what I needed to bring and do.

Then Alicia caught up with my uncle separately so they could speak about it together. That helped her a lot. Having another person to bounce ideas off and ask advice from is essential, and it comes back to how important it is to talk about this with people. It's not just important for people struggling with mental health to talk to people in similar situations; it's important for the caregiver to talk to other caregivers too. These conversations can be sources of great advice and support and also a good place to debrief. Sometimes helping someone can be hard. Knowing the person you love and care for wants to kill themselves is brutal, and you also need support to deal with that. It's especially hard if you don't understand it and can't come to grips with it – so go to people who understand and can help you.

Alicia discusses getting support from Shane's aunt and uncle

Once I reached out, I felt like I had a better understanding of how Shane was feeling. I was given advice on how to communicate with Shane in an effective manner when he was struggling but also when he had a clearer head. During these times, it was a matter of asking deeper questions like, "How can I help?" or, "What types of feelings are you having?" This allowed Shane to see that I genuinely cared about his feelings and I was there to support him.

I was also advised that just sitting and listening is just as important as talking. Simply sitting back and truly hearing Shane express his concerns helped me understand his situation better. I was able to be empathetic and validate his feelings. I was also reminded that I needed to take care of myself. Practicing good self-care was really important in

> ensuring I was in the better position to support him. By doing this, I was able to stay by Shane's side so we could go through it together.
>
> Speaking with Shane's aunt and uncle allowed me to feel like I wasn't alone and I could reach out at any time when I had a question or if I just needed some extra support.

ALICIA OPENING UP ABOUT HER OWN MENTAL HEALTH

Alicia has been really open about mental health as well. She's similar to my mum in how supportive she is and how open she is because they've both seen what happens when people don't talk about what's going on. Alicia has had her own issues with anxiety, and we worked together on becoming more open about it.

Being open actually helped with a lot of the stuff she was going through. When she started talking about it, the support and understanding that came with it helped her. She had issues and experiences that she'd never spoken to her mum about. I said, "I'm not going to be the one who tells your mum, but I'm going to drive you to her house. I'll walk in with you, and I'll sit right next to you as you talk about it." All I did was sit there. I didn't need to do anything other than just be there. I think that's such an important tool for anyone who's supporting someone – just be there. You don't need to do anything because being there *is* doing something. It's the most important thing.

Once Alicia started talking and got a few things out, I left her and her mum alone. Sharing and being open was so good for Alicia's mental health, and it helped her and her mum bond a lot more.

For context, Alicia was having issues at work because she had sent a topless photo to someone she had been chatting too. He screenshotted it, and it spread throughout the school she was teaching at. So many people were talking about it, and she got paranoid that everyone had seen it. Parents from the school sent her horrific letters, and she was treated differently by colleagues.

After talking through everything with her support system, Alicia was able to work through all of the issues she was facing. She quit her job because of what was going on, and I was able to support her. The ability to speak up has such a powerful ripple effect. After Alicia quit, her life got better. She has learnt a lot about how to deal with things, and talking about what happened was extremely helpful for herself and for others.

So many people get into that situation and are the victims of revenge porn or similar acts, and their mental states often deteriorate rapidly. Being open helps so much. It helps the person experiencing it deal with it, but it also helps other people know they're not alone and help is out there.

MY MUM'S ADVICE FOR CAREGIVERS

I've asked my mum, Sally, to share some of her experiences with me when I was growing up, along with her advice for caregivers, family members, and loved ones of people who are struggling with mental health.

With some mental health situations, you just get through stuff, and you just move on with life, so you forget things. For this reason, it's good to hear other people's accounts of the things you experienced. Here's what my mum had to say…

Growing up with Shane

Life is such a blur when you have young kids and you're so busy. Shane was a very good baby, which was lovely, but he had a temper – the 'terrible twos' were horrible. He was like the little girl with the curl: when he was good, he was really good, but when he was bad, he was horrible. When I had Steven, I was waiting for the terrible twos, and they never came. I was like, "Oh, this is different."

So, when Shane got a bit older, I was unaware of a lot of the stuff he was going through. But I do remember that when he was in year seven and starting high school, he did struggle a lot with kids bullying him. In hindsight, I think the kids were really mean to him, in part, because he was really sensitive. He would react to things, and, with kids being kids, they would play on that.

Up until then, everything with Shane seemed good. Because he was my first child, I didn't really know any better. Everything seemed okay. We had a good family life, and everyone was happy. I was working part-time, so I was there for the kids a lot, and they were enjoying life. I've got a great extended family as well, so we had lots of family time.

Probably the hardest part was when Shane was in his late teenage years. When he was doing his VCE (Victorian certificate of education) in year 12, he wanted to drop out of school. I'd had a couple of phone calls from his school from a teacher (and counsellor), who was trying to help Shane because he was really concerned. He was particularly concerned about the end of the year because Shane didn't know what he wanted to do, and that was obviously really difficult for him.

Shane's whole focus was to just get to the end of the year, and this counsellor was really concerned that he had no focus on what would happen after school. In September, Shane really wanted to leave school, and he and I had a meeting with the teachers. They said that Shane was so close to finishing and he should just finish the school year, but they could also see the mental health issues at the time.

Shane drinking was also a real concern. I dreaded every weekend because I knew he would be out drinking. Then he'd be running away from his friends, and we wouldn't know where he was. That happened a lot, and it went on for a few years.

We had a really open house, and Shane's and Steven's friends would come over and stay all the time, particularly on weekends. That's just what our house was. I had two rules: one was you don't wake me up. Two was when I get up in the morning, don't be asleep in my lounge room, because I wanted to be able to have my coffee in my own space. So, I'd get up on a Sunday morning; doors would be closed because everyone was asleep, and I would count the pairs of shoes at the door to figure out how many friends had stayed over. I never told the kids to take their shoes off; they just did it because it was home. They felt comfortable and respected the space.

One morning, there were 19 pairs of shoes at my front door, so I knew there were 19 kids in my house somewhere. They would all grab pillows and blankets and find somewhere to sleep, all over floors and that sort of thing.

Shane's friends were really good. They would sometimes ring me, concerned when he'd drunkenly run off. Then I would try to ring Shane to find out where he was so I could go and get him. That did go on for a few years, with them ringing me.

Once, I got a phone call from one of Shane's friends while they were away at schoolies. Shane had run off in Queensland, and they were really concerned. I was trying to phone him to find out where he was so I could get him help.

Shane didn't drink during the week, and he was better at dealing with his struggles during this time. When he was in a place where he wanted to talk, he got better at actually talking to me. Sometimes when I was worried and I'd ring him, he would just text me back, saying he was okay, because I got it through to him that he needed to communicate. If you're trying to support someone but they don't want to talk to you, they're not going to answer the phone. But I got it through to him that he needed to communicate that he was okay, even if he didn't want to answer the call. So, sometimes I would get a message, and I would message back. Usually, he would eventually tell me where he was so I could go and pick him up, or he'd go back to where his friends were. There were so many times when I went and picked him up. I know the running away was still happening when Shane was well over 20 because Steven is two years younger, and I remember him driving me to where Shane was so we could pick up his car – and that was a worry. I know he was gambling at the time as well, so there were many worries and many things I wanted to help him with but couldn't.

I had never been a big drinker but during the kids' teenage years, I didn't drink at all. I always wanted to be available to pick them up. And, to this day, I will only very occasionally have a drink, because I know someone might need me. I knew I always had to be available to go to them, just in case – and it was mainly Shane I had to pick up. Originally, it was about needing to be able to drive the boys if they needed to go somewhere, but I also knew I had to be on call. So, as a mother, I was always on edge.

When Shane was at home, I knew he was safe. But when he wasn't at home, I just didn't know what was going to happen. If it didn't involve alcohol, it was stories of Shane cracking it on the footy field or cricket pitch, or wherever it was.

As the years went by, I found out things I didn't know at the time about what Shane was struggling with. That can make you feel really guilty. But, in saying that, my sister has suffered with depression for years and years, so I grew up with it. I was forever saying to my mum, "This isn't your fault, you're trying to help, but there's something that's in her that she's dealing with." I saw my mum beat herself up about it for so long, and she still does. She's 94 now, and my sister still suffers with depression, and mum still worries. My sister has a great family and a great life, but she has this demon. So, I tried to remind myself about that all the time.

As a parent, sometimes you look back and go, *Oh, I wish I'd made that decision instead.* But you can't dwell on that sort of stuff because the outcome is what it is. I'm a firm believer that you just can't have regrets. You made the decision you thought was right at the time. Fortunately,

Shane and I were able to have lots of honest conversations as he got older, and he was getting more of a handle on his mental health. When he was more in control, we would have these discussions.

I used to go on a trip into the city once a year and stay at Crown. One year, I remember a girlfriend saying to me, "You can have a couple of champagnes, you know, Shane will be okay. He knows you're on your weekend away and he'll be okay." Usually, Shane was okay if he knew I wasn't that contactable. In this case, I was contactable, but I wasn't right there. In these situations, he could manage to hold it together a little bit.

Shane's suicide attempt

Relationships were one of Shane's triggers, so I was always on alert when a relationship ended. I knew, for him, the issue was deeper than a girl, but it became a spiral. When Shane tried to take his own life, it was at the end of a relationship, and he was in a really bad way.

When I got that call and it was Shane on the other end of the phone, relief washed over me. I think I'd been expecting that phone call for a while. Thankfully, when it came, Shane was alive.

I remember that day like it was yesterday. They took him to hospital and after I saw him and knew he was okay, I went to the place where he crashed the car. The police officer took me aside and tried to very gently explain to me that it was a deliberate attempt on his own life. There were no brake marks on the road, and it was obvious. Clearly, she didn't think I knew what had happened. "No, no, I understand," I said, and the relief washed over her face because she wasn't telling me something I didn't know.

That night, Shane was still in hospital, and we were at home, just sitting and dwelling on what had happened, when my friend called me and said, "Come on, we'll go out for dinner. We'll come and pick you up soon." So, they picked up me and my husband, and my girlfriend got out of the car to hug me. I just broke down and dropped to the ground. I was relieved because I knew Shane was safe. He was in the hospital, and nothing could happen to him. I could actually relax for the first time in years, and it was that relief coming out of me.

My sister was amazing too, and so was my family. When Shane's depression was diagnosed, my sister was really helpful because she has lived with depression for so long. She tried to take her own life years ago as well.

When you're on this journey, you often don't realise how much it's affecting you as a parent or the one who's trying to care for the person. Quite a few times, I had to fork out money that I didn't really have to help Shane, but, you know, you would do anything just to try and help.

Even to this day, when Shane's name comes up on my phone screen, although the stress isn't as bad as it used to be, I always wait for that first hello; then I'll know if he's okay. Because sometimes his name would appear, and I'd answer, and it was obvious as soon as he opened his mouth whether he was good or bad. Just the tone of his voice told me straight away.

I was lucky because Shane could talk to me, and he would help me help him. When he was good, he'd give me some tips for how I could help him when he was bad. Sometimes he didn't want to talk, and sometimes he did, which was really hard because, as a parent, you want to talk to your kids, and you want them to talk to you. You want to be able to help them. When he didn't want to talk, it was frustrating for both of us, and, because we're so similar, we'd clash.

So, I learnt the cues. I could say hello when Shane got home, and there were clues when he wanted to talk or didn't want to talk. When he wanted to talk, he would come to me. He told me that sometimes he just needed to be in the house and for me to be there but not do anything for him, just go about my normal business.

One day, after he'd moved out, he came back home. I was in the lounge room, and I saw him walk up the driveway. He walked in the back door and went straight to his old bedroom. I knew just from that he wasn't in a good way and he just needed to be in the house with me there, but he didn't need to talk to me. So, I kept going about my day, checking in occasionally and saying hello. I learnt that I couldn't ask him if he wanted a drink or food because he could do it himself if he wanted, and he didn't want me doing it for him. But that kind of thing is different for everyone, and Shane helped me figure out what worked for him. It's important to have those conversations and get that guidance from the person you're supporting.

Tips Shane gave me to help him

As the depression got further into the background or not as common for Shane, one of the things he brought up with me a lot was me taking care of myself. I always put other people ahead of myself, and that really bothered him. Me taking care of myself made Shane feel better, and obviously helped me too. I know, and Shane knew too, how hard dealing with his mental health was on me. It was really hard to cope, and Shane felt a lot of guilt about me not being in a good way. He knew that when he yelled at me, we would both feel worse.

Sometimes, I'd be at home with Steven, and Shane would arrive in a really bad mood. I'd ask how he was and how his day was, and he'd just bite my head off. Steven would look at me, and I just wanted to leave it. But Steven would be affected, and he hated the effect on me too. Shane hated it as well because he couldn't control that. He would yell and then go off to his room and feel really guilty, but he wasn't in a space to come out and apologise or talk about it. That would be upsetting. So, Steven knew what was going on, and we talked a lot, but he didn't really understand because he'd never suffered with anxiety and depression. Since then, Steven has had a work accident and got anxiety from it. Afterwards, he came to me and said, "I get it now. I don't know how Shane's done this all his life."

My prior experiences with people struggling with mental health issues really informed me on how to help Shane, but it was hard because everyone's needs are different. Many questions can come up like, *Do I sit there in silence? Do I talk? Do I leave? Do I stay?*

Being able to talk to Shane when his mental state was good was really important. He was so open to having those conversations about how to help him, and those conversations came from him. I learnt a lot from him about that communication because it was driven by him. By that stage, he was going to counselling and was on antidepressants, so he was working on it in other ways too.

Some people don't believe in depression because they can't 'see' it. They don't know how to deal with it. No one automatically does know how to deal with it, really. But having those open conversations when someone who's struggling is in a better place, to give you both that knowledge, is really important. You just have to try and read those cues, have those conversations, and make sure you're there for them. Regardless of what happens, you are always there for them.

My support systems (the people around me)

There were so many people who were important to me over the years, but there was also so much stigma that made it difficult to be open and vulnerable about mental health.

Over the years, I put up a wall to protect myself. Even 15 to 20 years ago, people talking about mental health wasn't like how it is now. Because I'd grown up with my sister's struggles with depression, I'd been around the mental health system a lot. However, there was still so much stigma around it. So many people thought that we should tell someone who's struggling to just get over it. That made it more difficult to actually talk to people because if you tried to open up to someone and they had that attitude, it was no help to you. You would just go back into yourself, and you wouldn't say as much, so you didn't get as much support as you could.

However, my family and my close friends all knew what was going on with Shane's health. Whether they understood it or not, I'm not sure, but they were really good support for me. They didn't know all the ins and outs of it, but they knew enough. If I was going through it now, I would share more than I did then. At the time, I took too much of it on by myself. Ross (Shane's dad) didn't understand it, so he didn't take the brunt of it, although he was still there for me. I did a lot of the emotional work myself because I just did. That was just me.

I still have issues now with not letting myself be vulnerable enough. I think I've been conditioned to be like that, and it's something I'm still trying to work on. My closest girlfriend is the person I can talk to about anything. Her son suffers with anxiety and depression too but not to the extent that Shane did, I don't think. Back then, I didn't share as much as I could have, so I don't know how much she understood, but I think she understands more now.

I now realise that I didn't let people help me as much as I should have. When Shane got older, he was taking care of himself, but I was still the closest person to him and still in a caregiver role. During that time, I didn't let people care for me enough. I did to a certain degree, but it wasn't enough. Back then, I didn't know how much help and support I'd need.

I think being worried to betray someone's trust when they talk to you about their mental health is a common feeling. There's also worry about burdening and hurting other people. You don't want other people to be hurt, so you try and protect everyone. Even with my mum, Shane's grandmother, she always asks us to tell her everything because if we don't, she worries we're keeping secrets from her. For a time, we tried to protect her from what was going on with Shane, my sister, and my niece, who struggles with mental health as well. It definitely runs in that side of the family, which makes me think there's something in everyone who's struggling. Both my kids are totally different. With Shane, there's just something there.

Helping someone through suicidal thoughts or ideation

Part of the difficulty of supporting someone with mental health challenges is not being able to take their pain away. It's awful, and you feel helpless. This person, who you love, is suffering, and you just want them to enjoy life and for them to see themselves as the world sees them. When someone starts talking about the world being better off without them, you can't understand that. You can try, but you're looking at it from the outside, and you can't fully understand.

When it comes to those close to me who have suffered, I see amazing people with many friends, great supports, successful careers, and the world at their feet. For them to say to me that everyone would be better off without them – it's something I could not grasp. I just couldn't understand.

In terms of stigma, one of the things that really frustrates me is when people say, "Oh, if someone talks about suicide, they don't really mean it." No. That's not the case. You can't say something like that. Some people are talking about suicide because they do want help, but that's what their plan is if they don't get better. So many things that people say about mental health and suicide can be quite hurtful, so it's important to be careful about what you say and who you say it to.

If I'm sharing, being vulnerable, and talking about how I'm feeling and how Shane's doing and then someone brings all this stigma to the conversation instead of being supportive, that's not helpful. I think this comes back to the people who are around you and what you share with them. One little comment can make you close up again and not share, so it's important to surround yourself with people who will be supportive and open and will listen to you.

This can be a fine line sometimes. I'm a really social person, and I've always gone out with friends a lot. I didn't want to bring everyone down all the time, so I was often in a situation where I was with friends while Shane was out at a party. I didn't know what was going to happen, and I was really concerned. I'd have my phone next to me, just waiting for a call. But I was trying to still be happy and have a good night with everybody. I didn't want to constantly talk about how concerned

I was because I didn't want to bring anyone down. I also didn't want the flippant remarks. "He'll be fine" is a common one.

So, again, the support network of family and friends is so important, but it's a difficult position to be in. For all the reasons I've mentioned, you don't want to be a burden, and you don't want to bring everybody down.

Taking care of yourself

Sometimes you just want to try to forget. When Shane was in the hospital, I knew he was safe. Because I knew he was safe, I could forget, and having that downtime away from the constant stress was really important. Not that you can forget – but if you know they're safe for that period of time, you can relax.

That feeling of being on edge, with constant stress and anxiety, really weighs on you, so being able to have that downtime and relaxation is so important. I hadn't been doing anything to take care of myself, and that was on me. I should have taken care of myself better, but I didn't realise that at the time. I was living a really good life, working full-time, and going out with friends on the weekends. I was really, really busy with the kids' sports and life. When I came home from work, we always did stuff. I was on the go all the time. I probably should have slowed down and done things just for myself, as I was still doing everything for everyone else. I must admit, I didn't fully realise this until the pandemic. I was living by myself during COVID, and I wasn't allowed to go anywhere. I was working from home, and people weren't allowed to come to my house. I really enjoyed it. I thought, *I'm never going back to saying yes to everything*.

I used to try to please everybody else when I should have been trying to please myself. I should have been saying no to things, and I should have done things just for me, just by myself.

Over the past few years, I've done a few courses through my work. Part of that has been meditation, wellbeing, and so forth. Meditation isn't for everybody, but wellbeing is relevant to everyone. Just being in the present and enjoying the simple things in life is so important. When COVID hit, that really hit home for me. That was when I thought, *If I'd done this years ago, I probably would have coped better, and my life and advice to others probably would have been better*. Maybe it wouldn't have been, but there's a high chance it would have. I was on the go and on high alert all the time, and it wasn't good for me. I should have had downtime for myself. I should have said to my husband, "I'm going to go and sit on a beach somewhere and read a book. You can deal with everything for an hour." While I still would have been on high alert for Shane, I would also have been doing something for myself that I enjoyed.

Shane and I have spoken about the importance of taking care of yourself. When we're going through life, we think of doing nice things for ourselves as being selfish. But they're not selfish – they're essential. If we don't take care of ourselves, we can't be and do the best for ourselves and others. So, when you're in that kind of situation, if you can find something that can relax you, whether it be for five minutes or an hour, you need to do it.

Shane talks a lot about making a list of things you can do to help you feel better, and I agree – think about those things that are important and make you happy. Think about what you actually like to do, and why you aren't doing it. Often, we get stuck in being too busy and not prioritising ourselves, but everybody needs to do those things that fulfil them. This is especially important for someone who's caring for someone else.

You aren't responsible for someone else

It can be a lot feeling like you are someone's lifeline. My sister has said, "I wouldn't be here if it wasn't for Sally, she was my lifeline." With Shane as well, I was the closest person to him and his go-to for a long time. Now Alicia is his go-to person, which is great. Once he met Alicia and we all knew she was who he was going to spend the rest of his life with, there was a bit of relief there for me because it became a shared responsibility.

One of the hardest parts of caring for someone is feeling like you're solely responsible for them, or more responsible than they are for themselves, for their safety, health, and happiness. That was really hard. I've said this to so many people: if somebody is going to hurt themselves, you can't stop them. They're going to make that decision for themselves. All you can do is be there and make the decisions that you think are right at the time.

An acquaintance messaged me recently through Facebook because somebody she knew had died by suicide. She said, "If I'd known, I would have been able to stop them, because I've had depression before, and I get it." I just thought, *You have no idea. No idea at all.* Again, that's one of those ignorant comments people make. You can't stop it; you can just be there to support them. That's all you can do.

On top of supporting someone, you have to deal with so many different emotions yourself, and that can be really tough. I think speaking to a counsellor or therapist would be really helpful for some people. At one stage, I spoke to a counsellor myself, and it did help. When you speak to someone, it doesn't have to be a psychologist, but sometimes just talking to somebody who is outside of the situation and educated in mental health helps so much. You're dealing with stuff yourself, and it has a massive effect.

When I was dealing with it in the most intense periods, there were times when I didn't want to talk about it. Although I couldn't forget about it, sometimes I just wasn't in a place to discuss it. My friends would ask how Shane was going, particularly when he was bad and my emotions were really high, and sometimes I'd have to say, "I just can't talk about it right now, can we please let it go?" That was hard for them, and I didn't want to upset them because I knew they were trying to care for and be there for me. They were my close friends, who I knew I could talk to but when I was in that high emotional state, I couldn't discuss it because it was too upsetting for me in those moments. I knew I would burst into tears if I started talking.

Like Shane would talk to me when he wasn't in a bad place, I would talk to my friends when I wasn't in that high emotional state. When I was in a better place to talk about it, I'd answer their questions and explain that I couldn't talk about it when I was in that really emotional place. They were okay with that and understood me. Honesty and open communication helped.

Coming to terms with not being able to help someone

When you're caring for or supporting someone and you feel responsible for them, coming to terms with not being able to help them, particularly if they're going to harm themselves, makes a lot of people feel helpless. You desperately want to help your loved one, but you can't, and that's a very difficult thing to deal with.

Over the past few years, it has been different for me. Shane communicating effectively about his struggles, learning and growing, and age and experience have all helped – it's a combination of everything. Even the fact that people are talking about mental health now helps.

Earlier on, I probably did have the thought that I could stop Shane hurting himself and that maybe my words would help. I think, back then, I thought that I should have been able to stop him. Me getting older, understanding more, people talking about it more, and Shane discussing it more have helped me develop a better understanding.

I think there's also some self-preservation involved because if Shane harms himself, I know I've done everything I could. I can't change anything that's in his control. He's going to do what he wants to do regardless. He can't get inside my head and see things how I do, and I can't get inside his head and see things how he does. All I can do is support him and let him know, every day, that I'm there for him. No matter where I am or what I'm doing, he is my priority, always.

It's a real journey going through this, but it hasn't just been a journey with Shane. For me, this journey started when I was a child, with my sister. So, it has been a long journey, and talking to people is something that has helped the most. When Shane was bad, I was able to talk to my sister, and she could relate to a lot of it. Those open conversations really helped.

Anyone who has a family member or loved one who has some sort of mental health issue will be on that journey with them. It's going to be hard, and it's going to be long. They're amazing people, and we love them – that's why we go on that journey with them. We *want* to be on that journey with them; we don't want them to struggle or suffer.

Even when Shane yelled at me, I wanted to be able to talk to him about it, but I didn't want him to beat himself up about it. I often thought, *Okay, this happened. We can talk about it. I'm your mum, and I still love you regardless. Now I need to forget it because we can't hold onto this stuff. We have to keep moving forward.*

REFLECTING ON WHAT MUM HAS WRITTEN

Writing this book motivated me to have difficult conversations with those who rode the waves with me. It was something I'd never been willing to completely face due to knowing how much shame and guilt I'd feel about what I'd done to others and how I contributed to how they'd felt.

However, speaking to more people about those experiences has strengthened many friendships. I'm nervous, but excited, about having more of these conversations in the future. They've helped me gain a better understanding of others. Through these conversations, I've learnt a lot.

CHAPTER 10

WHERE TO GO FROM HERE – MY GOALS FOR MENTAL HEALTH

WE NEED REAL PEOPLE IN THE MENTAL HEALTH SPACE

When I started writing this book, it was more for myself and my family but as I got stuck into it, I said to Alicia, "I want this out there. I want to help people. I'll do whatever I have to do to help." I want to cut through a lot of the negative noise. There's so much in the mental health space that people are getting lost in, like systems and unrelatable info, and I think we need more real, relatable people in the space, helping others.

Sometimes, readers of books like mine may be the caregivers or loved ones of people who are struggling, not just the people who are struggling themselves. Most of us have wanted to learn more at some point or have even been desperate for answers to help a loved one or themselves. We need people who have experienced mental health challenges writing these kinds of books and putting the information out there, to help us all.

People who struggle with mental health and work in this space, such as Matt Runnalls at Mindfull Aus, are some of the best sources of wisdom because what they're sharing is *real*. It's not waffle; it's not clinical, and they really advocate for people getting help in any way they can. It's the human touch and realness that people are searching for.

For example, young people now go to social media and follow people who share their honest, open stories because they want to find someone who's real and who feels like them. We need this personality in the mental health space because so much of what you find on the internet feels clinical and isn't always helpful. While the clinical approach can be helpful in many cases, we're often looking for personality, human experiences, stories, genuine empathy, and understanding.

SOCIETAL STIGMA AND SHAME – MISCONCEPTIONS AROUND MENTAL HEALTH

There's so much social stigma and shame around mental health. On top of our struggles with mental health, the stigma and shame add so much unnecessary suffering. The wider influence of our culture can be invisible, but we all feel it, whether that's conscious or not.

There are still so many misconceptions about mental health. There's an idea that mental health is invisible, which, a lot of the time, isn't true. There are often signs and symptoms. They may be so small, and they may only be there for some people to see, but there's quite often something there.

We don't always look deeply enough into mental health or think too deeply about it. When someone does die by suicide and people think about their last couple of weeks, they may recall that they were extremely happy during that time, which can be confusing for people who don't understand. Quite often, someone is at their happiest after making that decision, consciously or subconsciously, because there's something in them that relaxes as they enjoy the time they have left.

So, I think, on the whole, we've reduced the stigma quite significantly, but there are still so many misconceptions.

Currently, we're still missing a lot of education and important conversations, whether you're someone who's struggling or not. This means that when someone opens up about their mental health, the other person might really, really care, and there's no stigma and no judgement, but they might not know how to have that conversation. So, to the person who's struggling, it might come across as judgement.

These days, there's still some stigma around mental health issues, and there probably always will be. However, if the majority of people understand mental health, we'll all be in a better place as a society. The reality is, it's the education side of things that needs an absolute overhaul.

Personally, I don't think people should get free mental health help. Why? Because when we're given handout after handout, there's no accountability there, leaving little responsibility on the person to get themselves better.

We need systematic change across the country. What do I mean? For starters, we could research what other countries are doing because many nations *are* doing things to effectively improve the mental health of their populations. However, what this really comes down to is teaching kids. For the past few generations, we've been so scared to talk to kids about emotions. We've avoided the conversation, and that sentiment has stuck around. Why don't we give kids the credit they deserve? They're actually more intelligent than us half the time. I think that's where we really need to start, which means the school system needs to change. Schools and sporting clubs need to have things implemented that change the norm. I know people are trying, but we need to actually see the change.

When I speak at schools, it's quiet enough to hear a pin drop. Half an hour passes, and I don't hear a single noise from the students as they take in my story. They care, and they can see the same story in themselves or someone close to them. High school is when it all started to turn to shit for me, so I want to be able to give that age bracket hope so they don't become a statistic.

WHAT NEEDS TO CHANGE (IT STARTS WITH KIDS)

One of the most important things to think about in terms of your own mental health, and kids' mental health as well, is this question: what's fun for YOU?

It's so important to empower kids to take charge of their own minds. Let them have agency, and give them knowledge to empower themselves and make their own choices.

Something Matt Runnalls does that I'm really passionate about is teaching the fundamentals of emotions. Matt's podcast has taught me stuff I should have grown up learning. The next generation shouldn't be taught it at 34 years old – it's way too late.

Going back to making a list – this works for kids too. Kids can create a list of things that make them happy and every morning at school, let's give them half an hour to pick a few of those things to do. It might be going for a walk, a bike ride, or a run, meditating, journalling – all things that are accessible in a school environment. It could be free time for them to choose what they want to do, within boundaries. Obviously, you don't want 20 kids running around the oval if you don't have the staff available, but making sure there's an environment where these kids can actually do these things and learn to look after their mental health is important. This is a proactive approach – it avoids getting to the end of the day completely exhausted and burnt out.

Even things like teaching kids how to cook can be great for mindfulness and fun, while also giving them a life skill. Just having a half-hour class to give the kids space to be creative with cooking is beneficial.

When I was in the mental health clinic, I put my phone away for 20 hours a day, so, instead, I did art; I talked to people; I played music; we played board games – all things that help the mind, keep our brains ticking, and help us stay present and in the moment. These were all activities I enjoyed when I was a kid but had lost a bit in adulthood.

At school, we don't prioritise those things as much anymore for kids, so we're all lacking creativity. Now, there's no creativity for kids that isn't structured, but they need the ability to be free. Most kids don't work well with schedules, or don't follow schedules. If they're given the space, they often explore however they want. They need this freedom in the school environment, to do things on their lists and enrich their lives. We can say, "Here are ten things you can do. There are teachers in these spaces, so what do you want to do? Where do you want to go? Have fun."

Giving them choice and the agency to choose what's good for them is so powerful. Kids can play, entertain themselves, and get creative, and it's amazing, but we need to give them the space to do that. As adults, we often lose or forget to exercise that agency and creativity.

There's so much talk and research around kids with ADHD, neurodivergence, and mental health issues, and I think sometimes they struggle because they don't have freedom and instead have so much pressure put on them. They don't have the opportunities they need to be creative, so they feel trapped. That's how I felt during school – I was so trapped in a bubble, but I wanted to be creative. As an adult, I did eventually create a personal training business. Then I started writing blogs and, of course, this book. That's the stuff I really enjoy, and I found a way to make it work. When you've got this intense structure, where you have to do this, then this, then that, you completely lose sight of fun and what's enjoyable for you as an individual.

So, empowering kids and giving them options is essential, as is teaching them the benefits of certain practices. For example, you might notice that one kid runs every day, so you say, "Hey, have you thought about doing meditation? Because it could actually help your running." Or you could encourage journalling: "Before you run today, why don't you write about why running is important to you?" Then you can teach them how to journal, empowering them to make good decisions. You can guide them to options they might be unaware of, expanding their understanding. Let's teach them that these things can coexist and create balance, and each tool or practice can help another.

It's important to ask kids, "How did that make you feel?" Don't invalidate their feelings – acknowledge them in the moment and reassure them that it will be okay. Let's teach them, while they're young, how to check in and see how things make them feel and what makes them feel better.

My son, Ryder, always wants to play outside. He wants to move around and do stuff, and one of the first things he learnt to do was open the back door to go to his play area. He was barely walking, and it was an accident waiting to happen, but we let him do it because it made him happy and fulfilled to play that way. Really, the worst that could have happened was him falling a little way off the outside couch or the bottom of the slide. We wanted him to enjoy life. We didn't want to lock him up. We didn't want to helicopter parent. At first, we did consider other options, like buying gates, but we decided to talk to him and teach him instead.

We give him as much freedom to explore as we can. For example, in the kitchen, he knows he's allowed to play with the plastic containers in the cupboard. He'll put the containers on the floor and throw them around, which is fine. He's a little kid, and he has to do this stuff. It's also safe because they're only plastic. We know he's not going to be throwing plastic containers around when he's older. Right now, he just needs the freedom to explore.

These situations can be hard as a parent because you think, *Ah, I've got to clean all that up.* However, kids are going to do it anyway and I feel that once they hit primary school, it's all structure and routine with limited free play, so we want to prioritise freedom and exploration for our kids and guide them.

In schools, I know teachers who join in on the activities, often doing art or running around with the kids. This helps the kids because they learn how to interact with adults in more of a playful way, as equals. Also, if a kid is running around and starts to cry, the teacher is right there for them to talk to.

Often, kids lay low in the classroom but if you get them in their element, they feel free to be vulnerable and creative. Using words to teach them how to express themselves can be hard. Instead, we can create comfortable environments and show rather than tell.

Asking kids how something made them feel is so important. When a kid falls over, so many parents, caregivers, and adults just say, "You're fine, you're fine."

But, in the kid's mind, they're thinking, *I don't feel fine, but I'm being told I'm fine.* So, these comments take away their emotions, and being told that, especially by a trusted person, really invalidates how they're feeling. Instead, let's ask kids how they feel and give them that validation. I feel like we've got better at this with kids today, but we still have so far to go.

With Ryder, instead of saying, "You're okay, you're okay" when he's crying, we talk him through it. We say, "You've just fallen over, and I know you're probably experiencing a lot of pain now, but you will be okay." You grab them, and you hug them. It's coming back to creating an environment where they feel comfortable being vulnerable and talking about their feelings. It's teaching them that they will experience pain, but, at some point, that pain will go away; the shock will go away, and they *will* be okay. But at that moment, you're acknowledging the pain they're in. With kids, it's about finding that balance. You want to acknowledge their pain, but, at the same time, you want to help them see past it. You want to guide them through it. Getting the balance right is crucial.

I know a lot of my emotional suppression probably comes from hearing, "You're okay" or, "You're fine." Now there's so much info out there about what people have learnt about parenting, whether it be parents learning from their kids or people who're now reflecting on their experiences as kids. There's so much info now about how we can have these conversations with kids, give them options, and give them space.

I saw one guy on social media whose two-year-old son was using a nerf gun to shoot at his mum, and the parents would say no and just take it off him. They were really struggling with it because when they took it off him, he would just scream, so they'd give in, and the kid would do the same thing again.

Then they tried giving him options. They said, "You can either shoot at Mum, or you can shoot a target." Then they set up a fun target for him, and he never shot at them again. His parents empowered him to make his own decision, which led to him making the right one. Kids are quite intelligent. While they sometimes do dumb stuff, when you give them a choice, they often do the right thing.

They also learn by example, so we need to be careful as parents, teachers, and role models about what we show kids. Ryder sometimes sits on the couch, playing with the remote and pointing it at the TV, not because he wants to watch TV but because he sees us using the remotes.

We all make the best choices for our kids based on what we know. I've seen so many debates about dummies for kids because so many people are against them now. But how many 15-year-olds do we see walking around with dummies in their mouths? Kids grow out of these things in their own time. We put so much pressure on them to give up or change something, but, really, we just need to guide them, and they'll eventually do what they need to do.

MENTAL HEALTH STRUGGLES OF MEN

I see so many young guys struggling with the same shit I struggled with. I see them thinking they can't talk about how they're feeling and what's going on, so they play into the same self-destructive behaviours that I did.

Society has changed in terms of encouraging men to be open about their emotions and struggles. But has it changed *enough*? Men and boys still feel uncomfortable about, and can be discouraged from, being honest and vulnerable about their emotions and interests when they're not 'the norm', which is awful.

Alicia and I talk through this all the time. After our son, Ryder, was born and I went back to work, I was working 40 to 50 hours a week as a COVID marshal, of all things. I was getting verbally abused by people daily. I was called awful names, and they criticised what we were doing, and the government. This happened every hour of every day in that job, and I'd get home, and Alicia would need my help with Ryder and around the house.

However, I needed some time to decompress first so I was able to actually be there for my family. After being abused for eight hours straight, being run off my feet, and trying to support colleagues who were experiencing the same shit, I would get home and need 15 minutes. Instead of not being there for each other, Alicia and I openly communicate about what we need. When someone's tired and vulnerable and their shit is making them struggle, if you heap more on them, they'll probably shut down. Alicia and I want to avoid this at all costs, so we openly communicate about when we're struggling, feeling vulnerable, or we need time, and then we can come back together. We both get to do this. Sometimes I'll get home feeling good, and I'll see she's not in a good headspace, and that's when I need to step up.

In the world we live in, when someone starts being open and vulnerable, we instantly think, *How does this make me feel?* and, *How does this affect me?* instead of, *What does this person need in this moment? What can I do to help this person?* It's all about 'me', and I think that happens across the board. It happens more and more when it comes to mental health because people don't know what to do with mental health issues and when we don't know what to do, we always go back to how we feel and how it affects us, with no middle ground. When someone tries to be vulnerable and gets this response, they'll likely shut down and not open up again, losing more trust in people and society.

For example, with young men, they might try to be open about their mental health, but their friends will just try to distract them with a big night out and having 'fun' to make them happy, but that's not what's going to help in the long run. Being supportive, listening, communicating, and changing our culture are what's going to help.

JUST SAY THE WORD... SUICIDE

I'm not here to denigrate anyone who works in mental health because it's a complex field and topic, and we just don't know everything. But I've noticed a problem...

Many people who reach out to me mention suicidal ideation. When I enquire further about it, they get confused. They're surprised I'm talking about it. Why? Because professionals have told them that speaking about suicide isn't helpful and they should stop doing it.

I feel like there's a fear that speaking about suicide will compel someone to go through with it. However, based on my personal experience and discussing it with hundreds of others, speaking about it allows people to walk into a different space in their minds, where the suicidal thoughts aren't as daunting. Often, discussing it helps rather than hurts.

When we fear talking about suicide, helping someone is difficult. Each time I've spoken about my own suicidal thoughts, I've been able to move through them. When I haven't been able to speak about them, that's when I've felt the most trapped, burdened by the weight of what I'm feeling.

Talking about suicide isn't easy and will always be a choice, but the more we fear it, the less control we have. Those uncomfortable conversations can save lives, but it's important to remember that someone having those thoughts doesn't always have the power to verbalise them, which can leave everyone powerless. That's why I sit here, reflecting and knowing that my two genuine suicide attempts gave no one the ability to stop me. That was on me and while I can't tell others how to feel, I can say it wasn't their fault and I know everyone did everything they could.

As someone who has stared suicide in the eye and been lucky to survive, I can speak to the fact that no one is to blame. A suicidal mind is sick. It's a mind in severe distress and pain, and the pain becomes too much, which turns to a complete numbness and the thought that everyone around us would be better off if we were dead, even if they try to convince us otherwise.

I learnt that if my mind could get to that state, I had the power to change it too. As someone who has been in this space for a long time, I truly believe that anyone can turn their mind around, and one of the biggest steps towards doing that is having the space within society for these uncomfortable, honest conversations around suicide.

POSITIVE CHANGE IS HAPPENING

There are massive differences between how mental health was talked about when I was growing up and how people talk about it now. Now there's so much positive dialogue and change. I didn't know what depression was when I was growing up, but now I can talk openly about it.

It wasn't spoken about at all and if you were seen to be struggling, you were branded a particular way and put in that box. Now we talk more about it, and this is promising, but we need to do so much more. We still have a long way to go, but it's good to see positive change starting to happen. It's great that the conversations are happening and that there's more openness, but we need to advocate for people more.

That's what I want to do – I'm advocating for people who are struggling with their mental health. I'm advocating for kids so they can grow up in environments that support their mental health. If we all have these tools and supportive communities around us, we can all get through whatever life throws at us. At the moment, we're just leaving people to figure it out themselves, and that's not a solution. Let's create communities to support each other.

THE RIGHT TOOLS FOR THE JOB

All of this mental health work, at its core, is about giving ourselves the tools we need to deal with challenging situations. We all need that, and we all need guidance because it's so hard to figure it out alone.

The fact that it can take 6 to 12 months to get into a psychologist in Australia shows how far we have to go. It's great that so many people are seeking this help and support, but the system doesn't support us enough. The reality is that we should be taught that psychologists and counsellors are there when we're struggling, but they're also there to reinforce the positives and help us work when we're in a good place.

Hopefully, in 20 years' time, with all these changes that are happening, we'll be in a much better place as individuals and as a society. That's the aim. We'll still have suicide, depression, addiction, and all these mental health issues, but we'll hopefully have much better support to work through them and give us the tools to work through them ourselves.

I think the COVID pandemic has been positive in a way because people are finally talking about their mental health and seeking help. People had been battling for so long, and they finally felt like they could reach out. Maybe they were already struggling, or lockdown brought out their struggles, and now they're reaching out because they feel they're *allowed* to reach out. We need to go further on this – everyone should feel like they can reach out for help at any time. Hopefully, books like this will help make that change.

We all need support and help, and we need to feel empowered and comfortable reaching out for that help. We can't get through things alone. We must get better together. There's a better way to work through our mental health.

MY ADVICE FOR YOU: FOLLOW YOUR PATH, NO MATTER HOW WINDING IT IS

I've always had a love for psychology and how the brain, body, and mind work. However, you wouldn't have known that from looking at my efforts in school.

I have a photo of me from my year 12 psychology class, where I've got a bandage on my hand from one of the many incidents when my anger overtook me and I wanted to hurt myself. It had just been broken as well. I can count four-plus times when I've broken my hands or wrists in situations of anger.

That anger, however, was a surface emotion that hid the pain and hurt I was feeling deep down. I was hurting. I was in so much pain internally, but no one knew. All they saw was anger and rage – both completely irrational responses to what was happening.

The thing is, I didn't want to be seen as a 'nerd' or a 'geek' by others around me. I was so scared of what others would think of me. I left my happiness in the hands of the people around me instead of taking control and doing what I wanted to do.

I don't regret not following my instinct back then and going down a psychology pathway because I've still made my way to the mental health space.

It's funny – when we get a bit older, we look back and respect the people who put in the hard work to learn, study, and do the best they could to follow their path. I applaud them for following their true path, which was maybe less winding than mine, and, from time to time, I get a little jealous.

Today, I sit down and read books about the mind, body, and brain, and I struggle to put those books down. I love learning. In a way, I wish I hadn't cared what others thought of me growing up because I may have found my path earlier. However, I've built this whole life, and the life I've built and my experiences help me see what I learn now in a whole different light.

My advice for kids these days is to follow what you love doing. Who knows? One day, the people judging you may wish they'd followed their paths like you followed yours. Being different is a great thing. It's where you find true happiness.

My most significant piece of advice for you is to please follow your path and your passion because that's where true happiness is. Jealousy and judgement become things of the past, while compassion and the ability to understand becomes your new reality.

This is one of the reasons why I like helping younger people follow their purpose and passion, and understand their emotional and mental health. I want to give them the skills I wish I'd had, where I'm qualified to do so.

When that photo was taken in my psychology class, I wanted to run away. You wouldn't know it by looking at the photo, but I wanted to run as far away as possible because I thought it would help. However, you can *never* run away from your mind. It's always there, so it's much better to work with it than against it.

12 TIPS FOR MENTAL HEALTH WHEN LIFE GETS CHAOTIC

Before I conclude, I want to share some of the things that have helped me work through my mental health challenges, while supporting others around me.

Sometimes life challenges us more than usual, and it's important to remember the tips that can help us in these times. These tips can be easy to implement but if you or someone you know is struggling more, it's important to reach out for additional help.

1. Set boundaries

Setting boundaries incorporates what you say yes or no to. It can be who you choose to spend your time with and how much time that is. You don't have to say yes to everything.

2. Put your health first

Putting your health first doesn't mean not enjoying some birthday cake or beers with friends. It's a small reminder that the food and drinks we put in our bodies can directly affect our energy, mindset, and more. You can think about how you can incorporate balance and moderation into what you're eating and drinking.

3. Be present

One of my favourite quotes is, "The time is now, the place is here," and it's something that I think is worth sharing. Rather than worrying about what might happen tomorrow or over-analysing what you did yesterday, try to focus on where you are right now. Be present.

4. Be mindful

Along with being more present in our day to day, being mindful of those around us has great power. In difficult times, showing kindness, empathy, and compassion can dramatically improve someone's day.

5. Set a morning routine

It may be as simple as enjoying a coffee on the front porch, but having something you do routinely each morning helps you jump out of bed. Some find that 30 minutes of physical activity, no phone use, or journalling can be beneficial to their mood for the upcoming day.

6. Set a nightly routine

Not unlike a good morning routine, having structure before bed can help you get a better night's sleep. Have you tried no screens in the bedroom?

7. Keep active

You don't need to be a ninja warrior, but a few minutes of physical activity each day can help more than you might think. A quiet reflective walk, a light gym session, or a few star jumps during an ad break can help get the blood moving and the mind active.

8. Allow yourself to feel whatever you feel

We all have feelings for a reason. Our feelings are there to alert us to what's important to us. That's why it's powerful to let yourself feel those feelings. Then, once you're done, try to let those emotions go.

9. Be kind to yourself

Not everything goes to plan. The chaos of life can elevate emotions, so this is a helpful reminder to be kind to yourself. Perhaps a friendly, positive word to yourself in your morning or nightly routine.

10. Set goals, not expectations

Setting goals and actively working towards them allows for shifts and changes, while still moving forward. So, like I mentioned in tip nine, things rarely go to plan, and expecting that they will almost always leads to feeling like a failure. Embrace the hurdles and keep reaching for your goals, large or small.

11. Take time off social media

Generally, social media isn't great for our mental health, so limiting your daily social media screen time can have dramatic effects on your health and wellbeing.

12. Spend time with whoever makes you happy

Filling your world with the people who make you happy sounds simple enough, right? Give them your time and energy and reduce time with people who bring you down. That may mean you only spend time with a select few people, and that's totally fine. I'm also a big fan of some quality time by yourself.

CONCLUSION

WHAT MORE CAN I SAY?

I was left feeling lost about what to write in the conclusion. I mean, how do I summarise in a book decades of mental health struggles, depression, anxiety, and multiple suicide attempts, while trying to help as many people as possible, with a message of hope, with wisdom? My aim was to answer some of the questions people might have and give people clarity and hopefully just a little bit more understanding around how crippling mental health struggles can be.

Having nothing to write made me feel like I was failing, then it all came to me as I walked into work and the news filtered through that one of my colleagues, my good friend, had died by suicide. It was only three weeks prior that we both said to each other before ending the conversation, "Here for ya, call if you need."

Suicide leaves us with this ripple effect that we don't understand, and I don't think we're meant to understand. Grief is this dark shadow of questions and trying to make the situation easier and more understandable than it currently is. But the reality is, the situation is never going to be easy when we lose someone to suicide. So, I sit here with a rather large understanding of how that headspace works and how difficult it is to step out of that space when you think the only option is suicide. It's a space where you've lost your mind, lost yourself, and you think the world would be a better place without you. Coming back from that is a struggle so many people experience every day.

Even with the understanding I have, I still sit here asking, "What if I'd just made a phone call? What if I'd just pushed a little bit harder?" And the mind wanders even further… "What if someone else did something, would they be here still?" And, "What if they were told more information?" But the reality, the hard reality is, so many of these questions are never answered, and every single person is doing the best they can with the resources and information they have.

Grief, especially around suicide, is confusing, confronting, and completely terrifying. It doesn't just affect the families, friends, and colleagues of those who die by suicide. It affects the whole community, especially those involved in the mental health space and those struggling with their own mental health.

I sit here hoping you now have a better understanding of the depths of the suffering experienced by those who battle this illness every day. I hope, by reading this book, you found something that might help you on your journey or others on theirs. I don't have all the answers, and that's a really difficult thing to say, but I do have decades of experience living with mental health challenges. I'm a survivor who's lucky to be alive.

I sit here and think that maybe there doesn't need to be answers. While that's calming, it's equally as scary because when you lose someone you love, you want to know why. You want to know what you could've done to make things better. On the other hand, I know that I, and others, don't have the ability to stop someone who's suicidal. We can't save anyone. We can only guide them.

I know for a fact that luck or poor skill was the only thing that saved me on 20 February 2010 as I stared suicide in the face. That luck is something I'm grateful for, as it allowed me the ability to work through my mental health issues and live the beautiful life I choose to live today.

Even so, the pain never disappears. It's always there, so I ask every reader to step into the uncomfortable space and talk about the topics I've raised in this book. And if you don't understand, find a way to be educated, ask questions, and be willing to listen. I ask you to stand in support of someone struggling, to do your absolute best, like many have done for me over the years.

It's not about blame. It's about looking at the situation and accepting you did the best you could. Ask yourself, *What can I do moving forward? What can I do to make sure I'm in the best possible care? What can I do to make sure my friends, family, and society keep making strides towards a better understanding around mental wellness?* It's a collective day-to-day, week-to-week, year-to-year group focus on making those changes intrinsically, creating a more positive ripple effect around you.

As a team, we stand together to create change, and, to create change, we must first make those changes within ourselves.

Mick, you knew you were one of the first people I was going to hand this book to, and I'll never be able to do that now. I still remember your first words when I told you about the book: "Will you do an audio? Because I won't read it."

Love ya, brother, and miss you. This one's for you!

ACKNOWLEDGEMENTS

This book simply wouldn't have got off the ground without a huge team performance. To the team at Dean Publishing, I can't thank you enough for the support throughout the whole process. This book has been in my mind for so long, as I've wanted to help as many people as I can, but I didn't know where to start or finish. You came along at a time when I felt like this story needed to be told. You not only helped me but supported me as I shared some of the moments in my life that I'd never shared with anyone before. Now they go public, and the fear of that was nurtured and cared for by the amazing team behind the scenes.

My friends… To stand by and watch someone fall, time and time again, into a deep, dark hole where they don't want to live must have been incredibly difficult, and I never take that for granted. When I start to fall back into old habits or old ways, I remind myself that my friends stood by me, supported me, and cared for me at my worst, and, each day, it's important to be my best, not only for me, but for you too. There are so many people I could name who rode parts of this rollercoaster with me. Instead of judging me, you sat with me, held me, protected me, and kept me accountable. While I may not always show my appreciation, please know I'm so thankful every day that you didn't give up on me.

To those who walked away from me and set your own boundaries, I thank you. During the battle, I quite often thought others were the problem and when you walked away for your own wellbeing, it helped imprint in me that I had to do the work to get better. It wasn't on others to make me change. I learnt so much from the role you played in my journey.

My family – Mum, Dad, Steven, and my extended family, it was only in the past couple of years that I started to fully understand the impact it had on you as you watched me live the life I lived. While I was in complete pain at times, I can only imagine how hard it was for you to sit there, knowing there wasn't much else you could do. I know my extended family played an extremely important role in holding my immediate family together, which enabled them to support me as I worked through depression, anxiety, and suicide attempts. Without you all, I simply wouldn't be alive today and every time I think about how grateful I am for that, I cry with joy that I get to live the life I wanted. Thank you.

To my wife, Alicia... You and our two beautiful boys are the driving force that keeps me going on the days when I want to stop. You pick me up when I'm down, and I couldn't think of better people to move forward with on this adventure.

IMPORTANT RESOURCES

Power, Strength & Vulnerability –
www.powerstrengthvulnerability.com.au

MyndFit – www.myndfit.com.au

The Centre for Healing – www.thecentreforhealing.com

Mindfull Aus – www.mindfullaus.org

ABOUT THE AUTHOR

Shane Kelton is an author, podcaster, and personal trainer. Previously, he has been a support worker and team leader at PIYP (Power in You Project) as well as a Beyond Blue volunteer. Shane is a speaker with over 100 speaking events under his belt. He has also been featured in several publications, including *The Herald Sun* and *mX*.

Shane's own mental health challenges grant him a deep understanding of the struggles of others, and he aims to use his knowledge and experience to help as many people as possible. Through his book, he hopes to motivate people to have the uncomfortable conversations and start addressing their own mental health challenges or helping others close to them *today*.

While Shane is an avid sports fan, his greatest love is his family. He is the father of two boys, Ryder and Colby, and husband to Alicia.

www.ingramcontent.com/pod-product-compliance
Lightning Source LLC
Chambersburg PA
CBHW072048110526
44590CB00018B/3088